strange sea tales Along the Southern California Coast

by Claudine Burnett

Historical Society of Long Beach
Long Beach, California

2000

Editorial & Consultation:
Barbara Barnes, Julie Bartolotto, Loretta Berner, Kaye Briegel, Shannon Crucil, Karen
Clements, Diane Erdelyi, Darren James, Karen Harper, Sydney Johnson, Jeff Lawler,
Yukio Tatsumi.

Cover illustration: Richard Ewing
Cover design: Stace Aspey

Printed by: Seaside Printing Co., Long Beach, California

Photographs: Collections of the Historical Society of Long Beach (H.S.L.B.), Long
Beach Public Library (L.B.P.L.), First American Title Insurance Co.

Publisher's Cataloging-in-Publication Data

Burnett, Claudine

Strange Sea Tales Along the Southern California Coast / by Claudine Burnett; illustra-
tions by Richard Paul Ewing.

p. cm.
Includes bibliography and index.
1.California, Southern - History. 2. Legends - California, Southern. 3. Marine fauna -
California, Southern. 4. Sea monsters - California, Southern. 5. Treasure-trove -
California, Southern. 6. Long Beach, Calif. - History. I. Title. II. Historical Society of
Long Beach. III. Ewing, Richard Paul, ill.

979.49 - dc20

ISBN 0-9610250-9-3

Historical Society of Long Beach
P.O. Box 1869
Long Beach, CA 90801

Dedicated to my father, Edward Edukas, who loved the tales in this book that I continuously shared with him.

Also, to the many reporters who first wrote the stories found here, the newspapers that printed them and the Long Beach Public Library which preserved them.

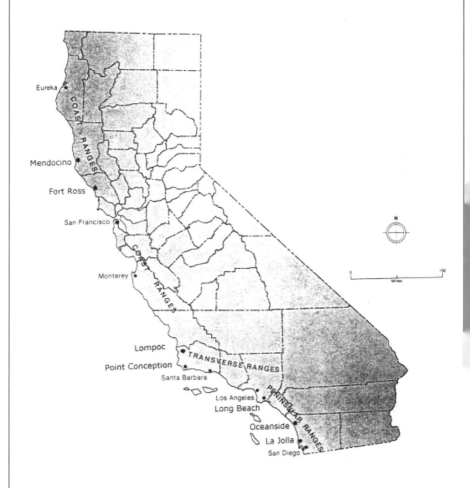

Map of California

TABLE OF CONTENTS

INTRODUCTION

Lying along Southern California's San Pedro Bay, twenty miles southeast of Los Angeles, is the City of Long Beach. Founded in 1882 by transplanted Easterners, the town was originally called Willmore City, named for its founder William Erwin Willmore. In 1884, W.E. Willmore, unable to pay his debts, relinquished all claims to the property which bore his name. The new owners, a Los Angeles real estate company called Pomeroy & Mills, envisioned a more descriptive title for the town. Suggestions included Crescent City, for the crescent shaped bay; Cerritos Beach, because the town was located on the beach of the Los Cerritos rancho; and Long Beach, for the long, and beautiful beach. Unable to reach any agreement on the city's name, each board member wrote his choice on a slip of paper and put it into a hat. The name "Long Beach" was the first selection and the one finally decided upon.

The new city grew, and in 1888 civic-minded citizens started a newspaper. When the Public Library was formed in 1896, it began to collect and preserve the early papers. In the 1980's the library also purchased microfilm copies of the *Los Angeles Times*, which began publication on December 4, 1881. These newspapers proved to be an invaluable aid in tracing the history of early Long Beach. It was in this treasure-trove of material that I found most of the stories you will find here.

It is questionable whether these stories are completely accurate. As most people know, newspapers have been known to stretch the truth a bit. In a letter to John Norvell dated 1807, Thomas Jefferson summed it up when he wrote: "Perhaps the editor might...divide his paper into four chapters, heading the first, Truths; 2d, Probabilities; 3d, Possibilities; 4, Lies." [1]

Newspaper accounts from the *Daily Telegram*, which existed from 1904 to 1923, are especially intriguing, and somewhat similar to contemporary tabloid publications. In response to what some might label "exaggerated journalism," a competing paper of the same period, the *Long Beach Press*, developed the logo, "If it's in the *Press* it's true: if it's true it's in the *Press*," which was printed underneath the newspaper's name in each issue. Surely, the *Press* was making a statement about the types of articles their rivals were publishing.

This book is the result of many years of digging into local newspapers during the course of my job as a librarian at Long Beach Public Library. Along the way, I discovered many fascinating stories. The selections here are my own. What I chose to do was write about things that I was amazed to find. Things that had once been written about but then forgotten--tales of sea monsters, strange ships, buried treasure and other wonders along our shore.

Enjoy.

Sea monster also called sea serpent. A fabulous monster of the sea often represented as an enormous snake that devours humans. The belief in huge creatures that inhabit the deep was widespread throughout the ancient world. In the Old Testament there are several allusions to a primordial combat between God and a monstrous adversary variously named Leviathan or Rahab. Although the references to Leviathan usually indicate a dragonlike sea creature, the name has also been used to denote a sea monster in general. Analogies to this combat are found throughout the ancient Middle East and also in Indo-European myth. In modern literature there are many references in poetry and prose to the Leviathan as a huge creature of the sea, including works by John Milton, Matthew Arnold, and Herman Melville.

> *Merriam Webster's Encyclopedia of Literature, 1995.*

There was a time when only native animals such as deer, rabbits, coyotes, fox, ground squirrels, pronghorn sheep, grizzly bears, mice and birds enjoyed the long beach which gave the city of Long Beach, California its name. American Indians from one of the villages in the region, Puvungua, Amungna or Tibahangia, visited the sandy shores to fish and gather seashells for trade. Surely they stopped to admire some of the indigenous birds--loons, grebes, pelicans, cormorants, herons, egrets, bitterns, gulls, sandpipers and ducks. Most of the Native Americans did not stay for any length of time, for there was only a brackish water supply in what would later become Lincoln Park in the downtown area of the city. The nearest good freshwater spring was a few miles further north in an area known as "The Willows."

The Spanish called the native peoples Coahuillas and later Gabrielinos, because they were considered Indians of the San Gabriel Mission. These Native Americans ventured out to sea in boats capable of holding as many as twenty people, trading with the inhabitants living on the off shore islands. At least once a year, mainland tribes traveled to Catalina Island and many set up camps for the summer. Santa Catalina had plenty of food within easy access, including tuna, barracuda, sea elephants and otters. In addition, soapstone, easily carvable into usable objects, could only be found on the island of Catalina, twenty-two miles off the Long Beach coast. It was a commodity needed by all, and traded far afield.

Since written records and oral traditions of these voyages are difficult to find, one can only imagine the tales American Indians told of the sea creatures they encountered. It would be left to others to write about the strange ocean dwellers chanced upon in the San Pedro Channel, and give us an inkling of what denizens lurked in the watery depths off the coast of Southern California.

W hat kind of an underwater terrain would Southern California sea monsters live in? Are there hills and valleys under the ocean for them to explore? Where, in the vast ocean expanse, would one expect to find the creatures? Would they be migratory, or make the waters off Southern California their permanent home?

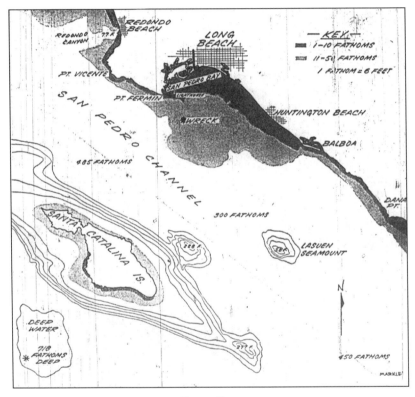

Ocean floor

Our local waters are part of the San Pedro Channel, which curves from Point Fermin to Seal Beach. Its depth ranges from 12 to 500 feet at its outer edge, 15 miles in the distance. The ocean floor of this channel is smooth and covered with sand.

One might notice something strange a third of a mile offshore, close to the Huntington Beach Pier. No reason for alarm. It is only a large rock that has breakers smashing over it at low tide, not the back of a sea monster. Another smaller, yet still menacing rock for seafarers lies a tenth of a mile off Newport, and from Balboa to Dana Point there is a whole slew of rocks close to shore.

One could chance upon some unusual specimens of marine life at Horseshoe Kelp, an area of kelp and seaweed 3 1/2 miles off the Long Beach breakwater due south of Long Beach. It is a favorite spot for Long Beach fishermen. Anglers from the Newport and Balboa areas travel to Fourteen-Mile Bank (the official name is Lasuen Seamount), a hill that juts up from the ocean floor thirteen miles southwest of Newport. This hill measures 5 1/2 miles by 3 1/2 miles with soundings from 58 fathoms to 250 fathoms, a perfect spot for sea monsters to hide.

About forty-five miles due south of Fourteen-Mile Bank is Sixty Five-Mile Bank, another ocean mountain, 9 by 5 miles, with water 300 to 1,000 fathoms deep. Another hill lies four miles northeast of the east end of Santa Catalina Island. It crests at a depth of 228 fathoms, compared with 391 to 428 fathoms all around it.

Redondo Canyon, three miles northeast of Palos Verdes Point, is a canyon in the ocean floor believed to be an earthquake fault. Irregularly shaped, it is 77 fathoms deep, while nearby the sea floor is 36 to 66 fathoms deep. Long Beach sea captain Billy Graves thought that mysterious gases from this canyon killed all the fish in the area in the 1880s.

The Gulf of Santa Catalina, thirty-three miles wide, lies southeast of Catalina Island, extending from Dana Point to San Diego. Outer Santa Barbara Passage, sixteen miles wide, lies between Catalina Island and San Clemente Island. It is here that Ralph Bandini spotted the mysterious creature he called "The Thing." Having saucer shaped eyes big as dinner plates, and a columnar neck and head lifting ten feet out of the ocean, how could it be anything except a sea serpent?

Oarfish at Newport Beach, 1901 First American Title Insurance Co.

One might not believe that sea serpents actually exist, but there have been many reports concerning them. In fact, a real 600-pound sea serpent was discovered and photographed in Newport Beach in February 1901. The *Los Angeles Times* reported that the "monster" was 21 feet long, and had a head 19 inches wide. Local fishermen said that they had never seen anything like it. Scientists later identified it as an elusive "oarfish," which never comes to the surface unless it is sick or dying. Thought to inhabit all the world's oceans, its flesh is so weak that it often breaks under its own weight if lifted out of the water. Hard knobs stud the skin which is silvery with a bluish tinge on the head. Also called a "ribbonfish," its body is marked with dark streaks, or dark spots. The eyes are large and the fins are coral red.

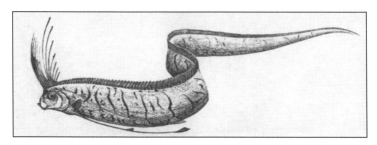

Oarfish, often mistaken as a sea monster

The dorsal fin starts on top of the head between the eyes and runs all the way to the rear of the body. Because the first dozen rays are long, it appears as if the fish has a spectacular mane or crest over its head. The internal organs are all packed into the front quarter of the body, so it can survive if the rear part of its body is bitten off. According to Bernard Heuvelmans in his book *In the Wake of the Sea-serpents*, the specimen that washed up in Newport Beach is the largest ever found.

There were many sightings of mysterious sea creatures in the early decades of the twentieth century. The *Daily Telegram* on March 11, 1907, in a story entitled "Peculiar Denizen of Deep Disports in Surf in Front of Bath House," described an interesting encounter.

A strange looking fish, at least fifteen feet long was seen enjoying itself in the surfline very near to the Long Beach shore. For about a half-hour, the mysterious creature frolicked for all to see, leaping out of the water and thrashing wildly about with his tail. The newspaper stated the monster was supposed to have been a young sea serpent. It had three peculiar bristles or small horns upon its head. Its tail was very long, splitting for a length of nearly three feet into three sections, each terminating in a pronounced barb.

In 1909, another oddity was seen at the local fishing banks when five men were out fishing. At first they were not going to tell their story for fear of being

Fishing off the Pine Avenue Pier in Long Beach, 1909 L.B.P.L.

laughed at, but after much debate they decided to risk ridicule and report what they had seen--a real, live sea serpent eighteen miles offshore.

The consensus was that the sea monster was about forty feet long, as big around as a barrel, with a large dorsal fin. It raised its brown head out of the water, and moved it from side to side like a snake. The eyes were the size of a man's fist, and the tail of the creature resembled that of a porpoise. One of the men was about to shoot it and bring it back to shore, but then decided he did not want to anger a creature big enough to wreck their ship. Perhaps the serpent got wind of their first intentions, for it started to chase them. One of the fishermen threw a lead sinker at the creature, which caught it in its mouth and spit it back so hard that it made a deep dent in their fish box. The men, glad that they did not get hit, put on more steam and left the sea serpent behind.

Another strange sighting occurred on December 30, 1911, when a big black object, moving westward as fast as an express train, was observed about a mile off the Long Beach shore by hundreds gathered on the Pine Avenue Pier. At times, it was almost completely submerged, and then it appeared on the surface traveling so fast that it only looked like a black streak. Old mariners agreed that it could not be a whale. Perhaps a submarine-type craft of exceptionally high power? Or was it the sea serpent that lurked in the waters off Long Beach?

In 1932, fisherman Ralph Bandini recounted his meeting with the "Thing" in his book *Tight Lines*. Here is his story in his own words:

"Some fifteen years ago--perhaps more--weird tales began to circulate at Catalina Island of a strange Thing seen out in the San Clemente Channel. Men spoke hesitatingly--fearful of unbelief--manifestly reluctant to attempt description of a Thing so monstrous--and yet, so filled with the wonder of that which they had seen, that they had to tell of it.

No one had been close to the Thing. After a day out on the blue sea famous anglers--others not so famous--would come into the club (Tuna Club on Catalina Island) stuttering, amazed. A stiff drink to steady jumping nerves and they would begin to babble about a glimpse, a flash, of a huge bulk lifting out of the sea--a something not unlike an upended hogshead, raising up sometimes as much as twenty feet! Of course that was pretty stiff to take--and yet, outside of its size, which might be excused on the theory of man's propensity for exaggeration, this Thing might be something more or less ordinary--a drifting, waterlogged pile--a huge seal--a sperm whale--oh--a lot of things. But there was something else--something that caused listeners to gather close--or turn away to hide their smiles--the Thing had eyes as big as dinner plates! In this all stories agreed! No one seemed capable of describing aught but those eyes! Great round eyes--rolling, staring--eyes like those of no other known creature! Here the tellers of these tales would talk defiantly, their voices raised as though to convince even themselves. It just could not be--and yet it was--for they had seen it!

Of course at first these tales were received with much derisive comment--offering a fertile field for scoffing mockery. Tellers thereof were solicited to confess what particular brand of whiskey was so potent as to conjure up such a sight--why all fishermen are more or less crazy! Pretty soon, however, the scoffing grew less. Man after man, all persons of standing, of responsibility, came in with the same tale and joined the ranks of Those Who Had Seen!

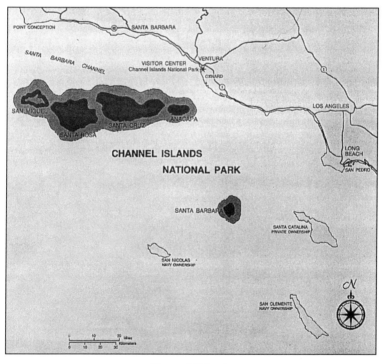

Channel Islands

A composite description of the Thing was prepared and forwarded to Dr. David Starr Jordan. That eminent scientist promptly declared it to be a sea elephant! Well and good--but if it was--then black is white and white is black and nothing is what it seems! I saw the Thing myself--and I know sea elephants when I see them!

My first vision was little more than a flash. We were fishing off the East End of Catalina--after tuna. It was mid-afternoon and very rough. My boatman let out a yell and pointed. I saw--just a great bulk, glistening like wet rubber, heave up an incredible height! Then a combing sea hid it. That was all.

It was two years before I saw it again--my second and only real sight of the Thing. We were at San Clemente Island. It was a little past eight o'clock in the morning. We were about a mile west of Mosquito Harbor and perhaps a like distance off shore. The sky was overcast--gray--with fog. The sea was glassy, with a gentle westerly swell. In that light objects on the water showed black. I was sitting up on top looking for fish. All of a sudden, out of the corner of my eye, I saw something dark and big heave up from a spot at which I knew I had just been looking. Swiftly turning I saw that it was something strange, unreal, bizarre, and scarcely a quarter of a mile away. Higher and higher it rose-- looking much like a great barrel, like a pile, like a monstrous seal. I seized the glasses. What I saw brought me up all standing!

A great, columnar neck and head, I guess that is what it was, lifting a good ten feet! It must have been five or six feet thick! It was wet and glistening! Something that appeared to be a kind of mane of coarse hair, almost like a fine seaweed, hung dankly! But the eyes--those were what held me! Huge, seemingly bulging, round--at least a foot in diameter--they looked more--and staring! I stood paralyzed, speechless, I could only point and croak hoarsely!

We had swung toward it--my glasses never leaving it, then I saw something else! There was not the slightest motion to the Thing! What I mean by that is that it did not rise and fall in the swell. Instead, the little ripples beat against it as against a rock! We were nearing it every second. The head, if it was a head, and I presume it was for those eyes were in it, had been twisting, turning, rolling around! Now it stopped. Those terrible eyes fixed themselves upon us in an uncanny stare! I could feel the skin on my back creep!

Then, even as I watched through the glasses, the Thing sank. There was no swirl, no fuss, no splashing, or other disturbance. Just a leisurely, majestic sinking--and it disappeared!

Now--I can tell you nothing more about it. I have related everything I saw. If there appears to be a paucity of detail, remember that for not more than thirty seconds I looked at something monstrous, unknown and unbelievable. If you should be so unfortunate as to witness a terrible accident, some horrible catastrophe, just see how much of the details you register. There won't be many--that I'll wager.

Only once again did I catch a glimpse of the Thing. Again it was in the Clemente Channel. It was in the afternoon, and as usual at the time of the day, more than a little rough. It heaved up out of the water, glistening like wet rubber, a good half mile away. Just up and down--that was all!

What the Thing was--or is--I have not the faintest idea--other than it was something unknown, unclassified--and not a sea elephant. I am not the only one who has seen it. Roughly I would say that twenty or thirty others have encountered it. Among these are, or were, Boschen, Reed, Twist, Martin, Mrs. Greenfield, Jump, Michaelis, and Farnsworth. The latter has had the best and closest view of any so far as I know. He was within three hundred feet of the Thing with very powerful glasses on it--glasses that brought it almost in front of his eyes. I do not quote him. For his description you must see him.

So far as I know the Thing has not been seen for eight years at least. Nor have I heard of it being found anywhere but in the Clemente Channel. I have heard of a similar monster in British Columbia but have no facts before me sufficiently tangible to offer. One consolation I can offer the timid--the Thing is very wary of human approach." [1]

For years the legend of the San Clemente sea serpent grew. Many claimed to have seen the monster, including several of Bandini's fellow Tuna Club members. Each of them saw it in the same waters: the Outer Santa Barbara channel between San Clemente and Santa Catalina islands; and each described it in the same way: a neck like a column, big eyes like plates, and a mane like a bunch of seaweed.

Was this the same creature seen off the coast of Summerland, near Santa Barbara, in December 1950? Opal Lambert, working in the post office, looked up and saw "something" swimming in circles about 200 yards off shore. She told police that the monster's head stood four feet above the water and that it disappeared after ten minutes.

In May 1953, the Fish and Game department received a report from Long Beach fisherman Sam Randazzo aboard his ship *Endeavor*:

> It was broad daylight and we approached within fifteen feet of the beast, which looked like something out of prehistoric times. It looked like it could tear up our nets so I fired two shots into it from my 30-30 rifle. We could hear the bullets thud into its flesh. It did not bleed but quietly submerged. It had a neck about ten feet long and five or six feet thick. Its eyes were

coneshaped, protruding, slightly slanted and twelve inches in diameter. Lower parts of the neck were covered with barnacles. Judging from the exposed portion of the body it would be as big as a submarine. [2]

It took Randazzo two weeks to report the incident, because he was afraid of being laughed at. Local attorney Jonah Jones, an ardent believer in the sea monster legend, was sure it was "Clemente Clem" whom he identified as an albino bull sea elephant. Jones took a photo of the beast, but all agreed the picture was so poor in quality as to make identification impossible. Jones told reporters that several Catalina Island Tuna Club members saw the monster and agreed, on close inspection, it was a huge sea elephant which seemed to make its way to San Clemente Island from Guadalupe in summers when there was a good albacore run.

October 1954 was a banner month for sea monster sightings. Barney Armstrong told *Fate* magazine that he saw a "sickly green" twenty-ton monster off the Newport Beach jetty. He reported that the creature was sticking up out of the water about four feet. The head was round, thorny, and seemed to have a kind of horn, like a cornucopia. Its mouth was two feet across. Orrell Reed, Jr., a passenger on board, thought the animal had two eyes, but Armstrong said there was only one.

Hardly less strange was an animal Phil Parker and Grant King saw that same month when they were fishing a mile off La Jolla. They watched the creature, from only fifty feet away, for about twenty-five minutes. They said the beast had a head and shoulders like a bull gorilla and no face. They were sure it was not a whale or a sea lion, and it did not look like a snake.

Throughout the summer months of the late 1950s, an annual sea serpent search was held off Southland waters, all on the lookout for Clemente Clem. Was the beast really an albino bull sea elephant or an oarfish? Was it the same "Thing" that Bandini wrote about? But Bandini was positive that his "Thing" was no sea elephant, or whale, and he never mentioned it being white. Perhaps it was an "oarfish." It did have big eyes and a mane. Or could there have been (and maybe still are) several unidentified monsters roaming off the Southland coast?

On foggy nights, strange sounds sometimes moan over Long Beach's waterfront. A *Press-Telegram* article in 1961 claimed the eerie noise resembled a greatly amplified dog howl. Coast Guard officials said it was not a fog warning, and Navy personnel claimed it came from none of its ships. No one can pin it down. Could it possibly be the cry from one of the unknown denizens of the deep?

In 1949, *Long Beach Independent* readers were shocked to find a front-page picture of a giant sea monster attacking the Pike. The caption read:

> Sea monster panics Pike! This astounding close-up of the gigantic prehistoric sea monster which panicked the Pike Thursday was snapped by *Independent* photographer Fred Wilson from the fifth floor of the Jergins Bldg. Wilson was on a routine feature assignment and had his camera close at hand when the monster broke through a section of Rainbow Pier and thrashed through the lagoon on the west side of the municipal auditorium.[3]

When readers turned to page seven they found that the Navy came to the rescue of the city by torpedoing the sea monster:

SEA MONSTER PANICS PIKE!—This astounding close-up of the gigantic prehistoric sea monster which panicked the Pike Thursday was snapped by Independent photographer Fred Wilson from the fifth floor of the Jergins Bldg. Wilson was on a routine feature assignment and had his camera close at hand when the monster broke through a section of Rainbow Pier and thrashed through the lagoon on the west side of the municipal auditorium. (Details on Page 7.)

LONG BEACH INDEPENDENT

Long Beach, Calif., Friday Morning, April 1, 1949   5 Cents

Sea Monster Attacks *Long Beach Independent* 4/1/1949

Prompt action by naval units spared Long Beach a major disaster   Thursday as a gigantic prehistoric sea monster broke through Rainbow Pier! Thrashing over a section of the pier that was under repair, the astounding monster flailed the waters of the west lagoon in the shadows of Municipal Auditorium, panicking the Pike and terrorizing the Spit-and-Argue Club. While standing atop a pyramid of his fellow beach gymnasts, Fred Sinew sighted the beast as it swept through the breakwater and approached the pier. Sinew somersaulted to the sand and dashed into a bar to phone for help. Capt. Bruce Galbraith of the animal rescue shelter sped to the scene and immediately realized that the fearful monster was beyond the powers of his troop, which stood by with nets and a sawed-off shotgun while naval units were summoned from Terminal Island. First to reach the scene was the Submarine Crawfish, which slipped through the break in the pier. Two torpedoes and a salvo from the underwater craft's 5-inch forward guns quickly finished the beast. Speeding to the scene Thursday night, Cal-Tech scientists identified the monster as a baffling relic from an extinct race of mammoth [4]

Some readers, conscious of the date of the article, caught on early, but others had to get to the end of the story to realize that it was simply an April Fools' joke.

The *Independent* was not the only newspaper with a sense of humor. Sometimes readers failed to realize that a reported story was to be taken with a grain of salt. In 1919, the *Long Beach Press* mentioned a letter they received from a psychic signing herself "M.M." This woman, who said she predicted the sinking of the *Titanic* and the *Lusitania*, claimed that a gigantic tidal wave would hit Long Beach on May 21, 1919. The mere fact that someone predicted the catastrophe was enough to panic many in the city, especially those in low-lying areas. Half the population packed up their belongings and headed for the highest landmass around--Signal Hill. Parents called school officials asking that all classes be moved to facilities further inland. When school personnel told them they did not take the prediction of a tidal wave seriously, concerned parents simply kept their children out of school.

As May 21st dawned, rain and a heavy ground swell made the sea appear particularly threatening, adding to the terror of the superstitious. However, the day passed with no huge wave swallowing the city and folks moved back to their homes by the sea. The next day embarrassed newspaper executives apologized for printing the story which was geared to make people laugh, not create panic.

Fish Tales from Billy Graves

One of Long Beach's most picturesque characters was William Henry Graves. Born in Kansas in 1864, Graves moved to Long Beach in the 1880s and worked in the fishing industry. A proverbial storyteller, Billy, who swore he never used tobacco or tasted alcohol, vowed that his tales were true and not in the least bit exaggerated. In one of the most interesting, he told of a strange incident that took place sometime in the 1880s when tons and tons of dead and dying fish came ashore. No one was ever able to explain the phenomena satisfactorily, and it remains a mystery to this day.

According to Billy's recollections, the beach was strewn with dead fish all the way from Terminal Island to Pine Avenue in downtown Long Beach. The shore beyond White's Point and Point Fermin was in even worse condition than Long Beach. In fact, the rotting fish became a menace to public health. Ranchers came to the beach and gathered the fish to feed their hogs. The fish included white and black seabass, (larger than any ever taken with a hook and line), halibut as long as a man; barracuda, tuna, albacore and small fish by the thousands, Graves told the *Long Beach Press* in January 1914.

Some attributed the wholesale destruction of the fish to a volcanic eruption somewhere in the subterranean caverns of the ocean, which was believed to have destroyed all marine life from Santa Barbara to San Diego. Graves said that medical men and scientists thought the havoc might have been caused by some plague which broke out among the fish, but they were never able to scientifically establish the truth of their theory. Strangely, when examined, it was found that some of the fish, washed up on the shore while still alive, had their vertebrae shaken loose from the flesh. This, if anything Graves felt, gave strength to the volcanic upheaval and explosion theory and perplexed the scientists still more.

One of the largest volcanic eruptions in the course of modern history occurred on August 26, 1883--the eruption of Krakatoa in the Sunda Strait of Indonesia. Could this have had anything to do with the death of the fish in California? The Indonesian eruption was heard nearly 3,000 miles away, and it was later found to have had global effects. Volcanic dust in the atmosphere caused spectacular red sunsets over the next three years in the Northern Hemisphere Katherine Cashman in the *World Book Encyclopedia*, says the volcanic dust may also have been the reason for a worldwide drop in temperature that lasted for five years.

Capt. W.H. Graves, 1909 L.B.P.L.

The first reference to this "Javanese Calamity" was reported in the *Los Angeles Times* on September 7, 1883. The article mentioned unusually high tides in California, which might be explained by the volcanic eruption. Reporters failed to make the connection, however, between the stunning red sunsets they were experiencing (they thought it was due to a fire in the Santa Monica Mountains), and the Krakatoa eruption.

Coincidentally, perhaps, there was much seismic activity in the Ventura County area following the eruption in Indonesia. On September 16, 1883, the *Times* wrote that Mount Hoar (it is no longer on contemporary maps), eastward of Santa Barbara, had burst into flames following an earthquake in the region. The *Times* reported one man discovering a cooled piece of lava that was "as big as a wagon." Another resident, traveling on the beach, said he saw clouds of smoke wrapping the hills, rising like a dark column into the sky. There were those, however, who said it was nothing more than a simple mountain fire. The Los Angeles newspaper sent a reporter to find out what was really going on.

On September 17, 1883, the unnamed newsman took a group to Ventura and discovered the so-called crater located in the steep precipitous side of the sea wall about a mile below Rincon Creek. Two or three hundred feet above the beach, the smell of sulfur was very powerful. In the side of the cliff was a rift or fissure, not more than three feet in length, and perhaps ten inches in width. Near the center of this was a round hole about three inches in diameter from which steam issued, but no smoke. There was no sign of volcanic action, nor any deposit of sulfur. A tunnel, running four or five hundred feet into the side of the mountain was discovered. Inside the shaft the heat was very intense. Though no volcano was discovered, it did appear as if some process of combustion was occurring beneath Mount Hoar.

Had seismic activity opened fissures in the ocean, releasing enough gas to kill the fish? In later years, oil was discovered in the Mount Hoar/Ventura area, as well as in the ocean off the Santa Barbara and Los Angeles coastlines, which would support this theory. Had this seismic activity been triggered by volcanic activity half way across the globe at Krakatoa? The newspapers give us no further clues. There was no mention of Graves' account of the dead fish in any of the remaining issues of the *Los Angeles Times* from August 26, 1883 through December of that same year. However, issues were missing. There was one positive result from this bizarre occurrence--Graves and other seafarers learned that there were larger fish in the sea than had ever previously been captured by local fishermen.

Billy Graves was full of sea tales, many of which local newspapers were delighted to print. In 1906, he found a monster sea turtle that was at least 20 feet long and 3,000 pounds in weight. He tried to harpoon it and bring it back to the mainland, but it managed to escape and live for many years (with the harpoon sticking out of it) about five miles from shore near the fishing banks.

From the size, it must have been a leatherback turtle, one of seven types of sea turtles (flatback, green, loggerhead, leatherback, Kemp's ridley, Pacific ridley, and hawksbill) found in the world's oceans. Peter Tyson in an article in MIT's *Technology Review* wrote that the leatherbacks have been swimming the planet for millions of years, but their numbers are declining. This is due in part to a loss of habitat. Also, their eggs are considered a delicacy and the oil from their skin an aphrodisiac. Biologists at Indiana-Purdue University estimated that the global population has dropped by two-thirds since 1980 alone, from 115,000 to 3,400 nesting females. Counting males is almost impossible because they never come ashore, preferring to remain at great depths in the ocean. As a result, they are rarely seen. The World Conservation Union estimated that for every 20,000 eggs laid, only one will reach adulthood. Though protected by law, poaching is still a problem.

Every so often, leatherbacks have been found off our shore. A 900-pound turtle was captured in 1921 and brought to Redondo Beach where it was put on display. The sea creature, however, drew into its shell, went to sleep and never woke again. Apparently, the turtle could not survive on the diet of potatoes its captors fed it. Today we know that leatherbacks rarely survive in captivity. In the wild, they feed largely upon jellyfish; Peter Pritchard in *Encyclopedia of Turtles* wrote that leatherbacks that are fed fish die even more quickly than those not fed at all, apparently from intestinal problems.

There were many odd creatures patrolling our coastline in the early days of the twentieth century, if Billy Graves' stories are to be believed. In January 1914, the infamous Captain Billy and a group of tourists sighted a school of strange sea creatures about eighteen miles southeast of Long Beach.

They were much smaller than whales, Graves reported, but they were still too large to be ordinary porpoises. Graves said the animals, which were from 15 to 20 feet in length, definitely belonged to the mammal family because spouts of water could be seen issuing from their heads. The captain, who got within 100 feet of the creatures, said they were big and black, like whales, but were different from the whales he had seen because they had a triangular fin rising from the center of their backs.

Tourists aboard Captain Billy's boat *Tourist*, 1915 L.B.P.L.

Captain S.L. Wood, a pioneer resident of Long Beach, thought that Graves might have bumped into a school of "blackfish," which belonged to the whale family. Though their habits were very much the same as whales, they carried their head much lower in the water, seldom showing it and causing a fine spray when spouting. Their dorsal fin was very prominent every time they came to the surface. There were several varieties of "blackfish," according to Wood. The sperm whale was the most vicious, with teeth up to eight inches in length. Killer and pilot whales were also part of the blackfish family.

Captain John D. Loop, who regularly led whaling expeditions from Long Beach, expressed the opinion that the creatures sighted by Captain Graves were "freak porpoises," for they were seen sitting upon the surface with a rocking motion, which was peculiar to the porpoise family. They were also described as having white dorsal fins and nothing like this had ever been noted on either whales or porpoises.

Ever on the alert for strange sea creatures, in 1915 Billy Graves hooked one of the most bizarre looking fish ever hauled from the sea. He claimed it was a ghost, or glow fish, captured about ten miles off Newport Beach. He told his tale to the *Long Beach Press*:

I had often noticed flashes of light in the depths of the ocean while trolling but paid no particular attention, thinking it was phosphorescence, or maybe reflected light from the sun, if the time happened to be daytime or from the stars if at night. But yesterday the light was so big and continued so long in one place that I brought up my marine glass to investigate and there, sure enough, was this fellow here, rubbing these two funny looking fins, or flippers, or whatever they are, together and this made the bright light which we all plainly saw about sixty feet below the surface. [5]

Graves went on to relate that one of his passengers, whom the others called "Professor," said the fish was of the genus "pyro." This species rubbed their tentacles together in order to make a light. This allowed them to see into dark crevasses and find fish upon which to feed. The Professor explained that these creatures were normally found in tropical waters. The only reason he could think of that would account for their local presence was some violent eruption of nature, such as an earthquake or undersea volcano, which would change the ocean currents and divert them northward. Captain Billy said he was going to keep the fish as a pet and try to teach him to light up the dark water at night to help catch other fish.

Devilfish

A swimmer, enjoying the waves off Long Beach in the summer of 1907 got to see an eight-foot octopus (also known as a devilfish) up close. Too close for his liking.

E.D. English was attacked by a "vampire of the deep" while bathing off Locust Avenue. The monster wrapped his tentacles around the Los Angeles man's body and limbs, rendering him helpless. English's screams brought assistance, and a fellow bather and police succeeded in freeing the victim from the clutches of the sea creature. When the badly bruised man managed to get out of the water, he had three bleeding wounds made by the octopus' sucker-like arms.

English soon recovered. He said he was swimming out in the breakers when he felt something grasp his leg. One of the arms of the eight-foot octopus rose above the water and grasped his body. English screamed and others came to his rescue. Later, they too, testified to the huge size of the monster from the deep. English and his rescuers may have thought the creature was big, but it was small for a "giant octopus." This species, which lives only in the Pacific

Ocean, has been known to weigh as much as 110 pounds and measure more than 20 feet.

Today, marine biologists view the octopus as a timid creature that rarely attacks humans. An octopus' bite, however, contains venom which can cause burning and profuse bleeding--it has been known to kill humans. The animal also has an ink sac containing a black pigment, melanin, which has been used for centuries for drawing. The octopus will eject the harmless ink into the sea when disturbed, forming a black curtain which clouds the water, permitting the octopus to escape. It is quite possible for an octopus to hold a man underwater long enough to drown him, especially if the octopus is anchored and the man panics.

W.O. Brown found out, firsthand, about the powerful suction of the octopus' tentacles. In October of 1911, Brown, hauling in one of his crawfish traps near Catalina Island, discovered two huge devilfish clinging to it. Trying to dislodge the monsters, he was seized by their long tentacles which wrapped around his arms, practically handcuffing him. To make matters worse, they also spattered him with black inky fluid.

After struggling with these devilfish for some time, Brown was rescued from his perilous position by friends passing by in a launch. It took awhile, but with much pulling, two men got the giant octopi to release their death-like grip on the terror-stricken man. The two specimens were brought back to Avalon and placed in the aquarium. The largest measured 5 feet 9 1/2 inches, while the smaller one was a trifle more than 5 feet.

An octopus' grip is tremendous. A two pound

"Devilfish" c. 1921 H.S.L.B.

octopus, for example, can pull with a force of thirty-nine pounds. They also have large brains and show considerable capacity for learning, as the Cabrillo Marine Museum in San Pedro found out. In January 1994, a giant fifty-eight pound Pacific octopus with twelve foot tentacles was accidentally caught in a lobster trap off the California coast. It could have been cut up and sold as food, but the owner of the San Pedro Fish Market decided it would be a good exhibit for the Cabrillo Marine Museum.

The octopus was near death after spending three hours on the deck of a boat, but Octavia (the unofficial name of the creature) managed to survive. Her new home was a 500-gallon tank about 6 feet wide by 4 feet high. Though her health improved, Octavia was not happy. After three months of being stared at every day, the lady octopus had had enough and she committed suicide. The intelligent female used her tentacles to pull a two-inch diameter drainpipe out of her tank. All of the water emptied out of her home during the evening when the museum was closed, and she was found dead the next morning. An attempt to revive the octopus proved unsuccessful. Museum officials were amazed. The pipe, which was glued in with silicone sealer and thought to be very strong, was lifted out of a fitting at the bottom.

Unlike people at the beginning of the twentieth century, who had little concern about the feelings and treatment of animals, citizens of the 1990s are different. Animal rights groups immediately demanded an independent autopsy of Octavia, claiming that the stress of captivity was what had caused the death of the sea creature. Earlier, the People for the Ethical Treatment of Animals asked that the octopus be returned to sea. They offered free use of their equipment and expertise to accomplish the task, but their request was turned down. After being told it would be impossible to prove a stress-related death, animal activists held a candlelight vigil outside the home of the director of exhibits at the Cabrillo aquarium, demanding his resignation in light of the octopus' apparent suicide.

Finger-loving Abalone

Other perils of the deep encountered by local fishermen, was finger-loving abalone. In July 1911, Clarence Brodie, diving near Avalon on Catalina Island, had an abalone attach itself to his fingers. He was held down so long he thought he would drown. Brodie made a mistake when he tried to tear an abalone loose by clawing his fingers under the rim of the shell. He was not aware that the powerful muscles of the mollusk could quickly close and trap anything in its grasp. Brodie was helpless, as the abalone refused to let go. Unable to hold his breath much longer, and afraid that he would drown, Brodie made one last effort to free his appendages. With one supreme wrench, he tore his fingers from under the abalone shell and quickly headed to the surface for some air.

Brodie was lucky. There are tales up and down the California coast relating how fishermen and others, groping along the bottom when the tide was low, had their hands and fingers caught in the terrible grip of the abalone. Quite a few drowned, caught in the rising tide. Some, fortunate enough to have a knife handy, chopped off their fingers or hand in order to get free.

Many are amazed to find that the abalone has only one shell. It is assumed that the abalone must be similar to an overgrown oyster or huge clam, with two hinged shells that close together like a covered box. But this is not so. The abalone has a large soft stomach and intestines which lie under the top of a single shell. Most of the "body" is a large tough muscle or "foot" which clamps to a rock. When disturbed an abalone grips the rock face, using its foot as a suction pad. The two main muscles of its body exert a tremendous force, up to 400 pounds in a 4-inch specimen-enough to trap a human.

Swordfish captured off Long Beach c. 1930 H.S.LB.

Odd Marine Life

Not all of the marine life off our coast is terrifying or vicious. More than a hundred kinds of fish, forty of commercial or sporting varieties, have been identified. They range from the broadbill swordfish, 12 feet long and weighing 400 pounds or more, to gobies, the little fellows less than 2 inches in size that dart on the bottom of tide pools. But several "odd" fish have been discovered in the waters off the Southland, including a freakish fish caught in the surf near the Long Beach harbor in 1935. A strange halibut-type fish was captured by O.D. Moorman in July 1935. Veteran anglers agreed that they had never seen anything like it. The odd creature resembled a halibut, but it was black on both sides, had two extra fins, a large hump on the back of its head and two eyes, one squarely on the top of its head and the other on one side. The fish also had two stomachs. Could it have been a Siamese fish, two fish sharing one body?

Sunfish caught at Long Beach c. 1930 H.S.L.B.

Another "odd" fish, with a skinny elongated shape, was caught offshore in 1957. The fish, nearly six feet long and weighing a mere twenty-two pounds was identified as a tetrapturus angustirostrus, otherwise known as a shortbilled spearfish. Marine biologists at the California Fish and Game laboratory said that the specimen, caught about sixty miles off the coast, was the first of its species taken within a thousand miles of the Pacific Coast. In fact, it had rarely been caught anywhere. The shortbilled spearfish first showed up off Japan in 1931, and later was caught off Hawaii, Florida, Sicily, western France, Formosa and now California.

In July 1955, odd "things" began washing up on Southern California beaches. The translucent, barrel-shaped jellyfish-like creatures invaded the shore from Point Dume south to San Diego. These strange specimens had Fish and Game biologists puzzled. The harmless creatures, about three or four inches long and two inches wide, were not jellyfish, but salpas. Normally they were found in colder waters north of here, and no one could explain why they had suddenly shifted further south unless there had been a change in the current.

Other Pacific Sea Monsters

French zoologist Bernard Heuvelmans' 1968 book, *In the Wake of the Sea-Serpents*, is considered by many to be the sea-monster-hunter's bible. It contains more than 500 sightings by sailors, scientists and laypersons around the world, including tales of our own "Clemente Clem."

Southern California is not the only place in the Eastern Pacific where strange sea creatures have been sighted. One sea monster was observed so frequently in Monterey Bay, that locals gave the fifty-five foot giant the name "Old Man of Monterey Bay."

In 1973, Paul H. LeBlond, an oceanographer at the University of British Columbia in Vancouver, examined thirty-three unexplained animal sightings between Alaska and Oregon since 1812. Many of these were mistaken sightings of ordinary creatures, others, perhaps, products of the imagination. Nevertheless, LeBlond singled out twenty-three sightings by knowledgeable observers that could not be identified as animals known to science.

LeBlond reported that one frequently sighted "monster" was "Colossal Claude," seen in Oregon waters from the mid-1930s to mid-1950s. Claude was said to have a head like a camel's and fur that was coarse and gray. He also had glassy eyes and a bent snout. There was also a creature observed in Dungeness Spit, Washington in 1961. Its body was a rich, deep brown with large reticulations of bright, burnt orange. It had a six-foot neck, three humps and a long, floppy mane. In 1951, a forty-foot grayish-green creature with something resembling a cod fish's fin (prickly and about one foot in depth running the full length of the back), was seen by fishermen.

In December 1992, LeBlond and fellow marine biologist Edward Bousfield presented a paper to the American Society of Zoologists documenting their findings. They reported a creature they called Cadborosaurus (after the bay where it was frequently seen), was discovered in the stomach of a sperm whale in 1937. The ten-foot creature was photographed and sent to the Field Museum in Chicago. However, there are no records of it there. Nearly every eyewitness reported the same sort of thing: a long, serpentine creature with a small, horse-like head, a coiled neck and a humped back. They gave Cadborosaurus an odd mixture of reptilian and mammalian features: needle-like teeth, a scaly back and muscles that ripple like a python's when it swam, along with whiskers, hairs and a whale-like horizontal fluke, rather than a tail. A baby Cadborosaurus was caught in a net in 1968, but the Canadian whaler who trapped it was so distressed by its squalling that he felt he had to let it go. These are all fascinating reports, but inconclusive until some physical evidence surfaces.

Statistician Charles Paxton of Oxford University used numbers to search for the likelihood of sea monsters. No underwater cameras or robot submarines for him. By studying the discovery of previously unknown specimens through the years, Paxton concluded it was unlikely, though possible, that an entirely new kind of sea monster awaits discovery.

El Niño

By the 1990s, scientists discovered a condition that altered our currents and weather--El Niño. This change in the weather pattern warmed up our local waters and brought in varieties of fish and ocean mammals not normally seen in our area. El Niño existed in the past, explaining some of the strange creatures seen in earlier times, but no one ever thought to track it until the 1990s.

The winter of 1997-98 was a landmark year for El Niño, bringing 29.41 inches of rain to Long Beach compared to 12.13 inches for a normal season. Scientists estimated $32 billion in damages worldwide from the 1997-98 phenomenon, and 23,000 deaths. It also brought all sorts of unusual visitors to Southland waters. On February 18, 1998, a rare, dead, fourteen-foot-long dense beaked whale washed ashore in Newport Beach. The male was one of a relatively new species never before seen in California--a Peruvian beaked whale. About thirteen specimens of this whale, which has two tusk-like teeth protruding from its lower jaw, have been found worldwide, according to Los Angeles County Natural History Museum officials.

Another type of beaked whale, a North Pacific type, was mistaken for a sea serpent when it washed up on the rocks at Santa Cruz, California in 1925. It was a strange creature with a huge head longer than a man, tiny eyes and a sort of duck's beak. It was joined to the main body by a slender neck that seemed to be about 30-feet long. The specimen was 36 feet 6 inches long.

66. Santa Cruz carcase, 1925

Sea Serpent, 1925 (Photo reproduced from *Santa Cruz Sentinel* 1/4/1989)

Apparently the effect of decomposition and heavy seas separated the body from the skin, giving the illusion of a long neck joined to the body.

The entire marine-mammal community in Southern California was excited about the strange species of marine mammals and fish brought to our coast by El Niño. Another warm-water whale, the pygmy sperm whale, was captured alive on January 19, 1998 in Alamitos Bay in Long Beach. It died, however, while being transported to Sea World in San Diego.

February 1998 proved to be the wettest month in Southern California history (since the Weather Bureau started keeping track of the weather back in 1877). As a result, there were disastrous landslides and floods. Warmer waters brought north by El Niño meant less food for the seal population, which started to die of starvation. But not all of El Niño was bad. There was one benefit of having warmer waters--an increase in the lobster population.

By October of 1997, Newport Beach based fishermen were used to their decks sagging from the weight of capacity lobster catches. An unbelievable five tons of lobsters were pulled from Southland waters between July and October. Marine biologists attributed the big catch, in part, to prior El Niños--the strong one in 1983 and the milder, fluctuating El Niño effect of 1991 through 1995. They theorized that the warmer waters brought more food for baby lobsters and the current also carried some young lobsters north from Mexican waters. Big ocean swells helped wash the crustaceans from their hiding places and increased the chance that they would mistake the mackerel-baited fish traps used by fishermen for a nice new home already stocked with food.

The last big lobster haul occurred in 1950, when the total catch for the season was 900,000 pounds. Over harvesting of the spiny crustacean in the 1960s severely decreased the lobster population off our coast. In the late 1990s, El Niño was bringing the succulent sea creature back to its former numbers, and lowering the price for this delicacy.

Happy anglers, July 21, 1896 H.S.L.B.

No one alive today can resist the spell cast by the playful sea otter. The furry creatures always seem to be enjoying themselves, and their enthusiasm for whatever they are doing is contagious. But our forefathers in the nineteenth century saw only dollar signs from the warm, downy fur of the sea otter. As a result, the friendly mammal was hunted down and killed for its coat. By the beginning of the 20th century, the sea otter was so rare that its pelts were regarded as the most valuable of all furs. Today, the playful otter is just beginning to resurface in local waters.

The Hunt

Otter hunting was an exciting and dangerous activity during the mission days of California (1769-1833). The Spanish traded the highly valued pelts in the Orient, sending them across the Pacific in their Manila galleons. Native Americans were encouraged to hunt for otter, bringing the fur to the missions, in exchange for goods and supplies. The Mission fathers, in turn, turned the pelts over to the viceroy of New Spain for eastern trade.

Spanish officials, anxious to keep the riches of California and her coast to themselves, were determined that sea otter furs could not be sold or traded except to and by the Mission fathers. But the strength of its army did not help the Spaniards, for foreign hunters turned to smuggling. Between 1795 and 1812, American ship captains worked in partnership with the Russians in hunting otters and trying to outwit the Spanish. Sailing ships met fishermen and Indians at sea and traders bought the pelts from them.

The earliest otter hunters were the Aleuts from the Aleutian Islands off Alaska. They used light skin boats called "bidarkas" to pursue their prey. The Alaskan natives wore waterproof clothing and wooden hats decorated with sea lion whiskers. The harpoon was their weapon of choice. The Russians employed these Alaskan natives to help them in the hunt, but as the otter population off Alaska dwindled, the Russians moved south taking some of the Aleutian natives with them.

In 1812, the Russians built Fort Ross located north of San Francisco Bay, far away from the Spanish, turning it into a base for their otter hunting operations. They established hunter-colonies on California's offshore islands. The Aleuts lived on these islands year round, gathering otter pelts in anticipation of the yearly visits by the Russians to collect the furs. The Americans began to work independently, hiring natives from the Sandwich (Hawaiian) Islands. During the 1830s, the Aleuts had many battles with Americans and with helpless natives over choice hunting grounds in Southern California's Channel Islands.

In November 1883, the *Los Angeles Times* published a first hand account of otter hunting in the Santa Barbara Channel. In fact, at that time about the only place one could still find the otter in southern waters was among the Santa Barbara Islands. The valuable mammal once ranged along the Pacific Coast in vast numbers from Alaska all the way to Lower California. San Nicolas Island, one of the Channel Islands, was originally given the name Sea Otter Island because of the great number of sea otters once found there.

The Aleuts used from five to twenty of their canoes to hunt otter. Keeping their canoes spread out in a long line, they paddled about, muffling each dip of their oars to keep as quiet as possible. Once an otter was sighted the group circled the animal, maneuvering their boats to cover the areas where the animal might be expected to resurface. The native nearest the spot where the otter rose would give a wild shout in an attempt to force the otter to dive before it could completely fill its lungs with air. At the same time, the Aleut threw his arrow at the disappearing animal. A second circle then formed, and the chase continued until the exhausted and wounded creature was finally caught.

By 1883, otter tracking had changed. Guns were used and at least three men, good at shooting and rowing, were put into several small boats. It was helpful if at least one of them had a good eye, someone that could tell the difference between an otter and a sea gull at a distance. Like the Aleuts before them, an intrepid otter stalker of the 1880s had to have a lot of patience.

These furry creatures were swift swimmers, traveling in groups of seventy five to a hundred. They liked to float on their backs by the hour among the kelp beds, but once fired upon they would dive and stay under for what seemed like forever. An otter hunter from the 1880s would say that the creature could remain under the water without air for more than an hour. Today we know that is not true. The longest submergence on record for an otter, according to *The New International Wildlife Encyclopedia*, is four minutes and twenty-five seconds.

A hunter had to guess where the otter might surface next, something that was not easy to do. However, the time spent in tracking the creature was well worth it. Once caught and skinned, an otter pelt could bring up to $500 on the wholesale market. Quite a tidy sum for one sea otter, which explains why they are not around much any more.

In 1915, Captain Charles Matson told the *Long Beach Press* an interesting story with roots dating back to the early days of otter hunting. Matson told the newspaper he had recently been forced to find shelter from an approaching storm at San Miguel Island. The island, the most westerly of the Santa Barbara group, was treeless but covered with coarse grass and massive sand dunes. While camped on the sandy beach, gale-force winds kept Matson and his men up most of the night. When the crew woke up the next morning, they found a number of uncovered skeletons close to their camp. The skeletons apparently were those of a race of giant Indians. Digging further into the sand, the men unearthed forty skeletons, some complete and fairly well preserved with thighbones much larger and heavier than normal men. Believing they would be an interesting attraction in a carnival sideshow, Matson brought two of the skeletons back to Long Beach and sold them.

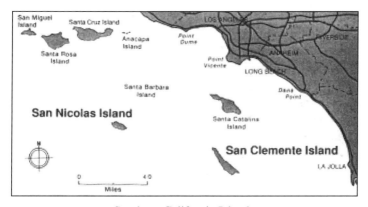

Southern California Islands

While on San Miguel, Matson spoke with an old man and his wife, who farmed on the island for a number of years. The rancher said he too had uncovered a number of skeletons on various parts of the island, but never in such large numbers as Matson. Where did these skeletons originally come from? Perhaps one answer can be found in the fact that many people believed the Spanish explorer Cabrillo was buried at Cuyler's Harbor on San Miguel. It was said that the conquistador was interred in full armor made of polished gold. Many treasure seeker dug on the island searching for the remains of the great discoverer and for his valuable suit of armor. Could it be that during the search for Cabrillo and his fabled suit of gold, these skeletons were dug up from lower depths and left on the surface by treasure hunters?

The farmer had a second theory. He recalled a story that the skeletons were those of a once powerful and warlike band, exterminated by Russian otter hunters and fishermen who swooped down on the island in the early 1800s. Some of the tribe members were said to have survived, being carried away into captivity by the Russians. Perhaps the San Miguel rancher had his story confused with what happened on neighboring San Nicolas Island, or conceivably, the Russians may have also murdered the native inhabitants of San Miguel. It is known that the Russians used to visit the islands in quest of sea otter pelts. They brought with them natives from Alaska who were left on the islands to continue the work of capturing otters while the Russians returned to the north. During the Russians' absence, these Alaska Indians, having been taught the use of firearms, took possession of all the women on San Nicolas Island. In the conflict that followed, the entire male population, including young boys, were killed. When the Russian ships came again, they took away the Alaskans and the women were abandoned to their fate. The news of the massacre reached the Mission fathers on the mainland and in 1835, the priests dispatched a schooner to San Nicolas Island to bring back the remaining inhabitants. One woman, however, was left behind There she lived, by herself, until 1853 when a ship landed and rescued her. Her tale was later told in Scott Odell's book *Island of the Blue Dolphins* and its sequel *Zia*.

Hope

Like the rescued woman on San Nicolas Island, the otter population was also saved. In 1910, the United States government introduced a law prohibiting the capture of the furry mammal within American waters. Soon other interested governments followed, but it would take years to undo the damage done by over hunting.

By 1998, the playful creatures found their way back to the Channel Islands but fishermen were not happy. Because of a high metabolic rate necessary to keep warm in the cold waters of the Pacific Ocean, an otter, which weighs from 10 to 25 pounds when grown, eats from a quarter to a third of its body weight every day. Fishermen do not like the competition.

Under a 1986 law (PL99-625) the U.S. Fish and Wildlife Service was charged with relocating any otters that migrated south of Point Conceptio (located about twelve miles southeast of Lompoc). This was because a federal "no otter" boundary was established to protect the shellfish industry. In 1998, group of about 100 young male sea otters expanded their range south into Sant Barbara County, crossing the "no otter" zone.

The Fish and Wildlife Service found themselves in a tight spot. Both the otter lovers and the fishermen were vocal advocates for their causes. If they killed any otters during relocation, the federal agency would be in trouble. If the otters were allowed to stay, Santa Barbara's marine ecosystem--which supports an abundance of sea urchins, crab, lobster and a recovering abalone population-- would change. When the predatory otters were present, shellfish populations plummeted below harvestable levels. This meant big losses for commercial fishermen.

The "no otter" zone south of Point Conception was approved by the government as mitigation for a plan to create a colony of otters on San Nicolas Island. The intent was to establish a small sea otter colony there in case an oil spill wiped out the larger population to the north. But putting otters on the island once known as Sea Otter Island meant the end of the lucrative shellfish industry there. In exchange, the government pledged that otters would not be allowed to expand into the fishing grounds south of Point Conception. In the end, the otters did not thrive on San Nicolas, possibly because of a food shortage caused by El Niño, and they moved south. Up until now, Fish and Wildlife officials say they do not know what they will do and have set no timetable for making an announcement. They have acknowledged, however, the lack of necessary funds to relocate the otters.

It appears that nature has also stepped into the picture. A twice-yearly survey released in December of 1998 showed 1,937 otters along the 300 miles of California coastline. This was a twelve percent decrease since the fall of 1997, and the fewest otters since a record high of 2,377 in the spring of 1995. Scientists fear that the decline may signal a new danger for the health of the species. They are looking into possible causes including pollution and disease. The only certainty is that if subsequent counts drop below 1,850, the otters' designation on the Endangered Species List will shift from threatened to endangered.

The recovering otter population of Alaska has also fallen, the reason being an imbalance in the ecosystem. Orcas, also known as killer whales, have begun eating the otters after centuries of peaceful coexistence. This is all because of a complicated food chain. Ocean fish declined in the Pacific Northwest because the sea urchin population exploded. The urchins devoured the kelp forests, which fed the oily, nutritious ocean perch and herring. Consequently, sea lions and seals, which fed on the fish and are the principle food of the killer whales, declined in numbers. The whales now eat the sea otters, which keep the sea urchin population in check. This vicious circle will continue until the ecosystem regains balance.

An appropriate mascot for the City of Long Beach would be the whale. Whales have always played an important part in the history of this city as the following stories will show. Some of the tales may appear cruel when looked at by today's standards. Fortunately we no longer hunt whales with harpoons or bombs, but with cameras and compassion. At the beginning of the twentieth century, whales and other creatures were viewed as sport to be hunted, not preserved for environmental and humane purposes. Some of these stories may appear far-fetched, but they did all appear in the press. At least no one claimed to have seen a white whale, like Moby Dick, patrolling the waters off our coast. However, there was an albino dolphin.

"Minnie" the Municipal Whale or the Library?

It is hard for us to envision what a curiosity a whale was to the general public at the turn of the century. Seeing a whale then would be similar to encountering a live dinosaur today. Long Beach folk particularly loved the municipal whale which first washed up on the shore in 1897. It was a tourist draw, bringing prosperity to the seaside resort.

The sixty-three foot whale was wounded, perhaps, by two young men who were firing rifles from a boat not far from shore a few days earlier. People came

Long Beach's first tourist attraction, 1897 H.S.L.B.

HEAVING UP JONAH,
WHALE, CAPTURED AT LONG BEACH CAL.
LENGTH 63 FT.
CJ DAUGHERTY
NO114. PHOTO

Sixty-three foot whale, 1897 H.S.L.B.

from all around to view the whale that died shortly thereafter. Astute businessmen, seeing the popularity of this denizen of the deep, decided to boil the carcass down and mount the skeleton in Lincoln Park.

People flocked to Long Beach to see the town's first tourist attraction. In 1919, when the Chamber of Commerce wanted to advertise Long Beach by exhibiting the whale skeleton throughout the Midwest, City Commissioners refused. They said the whale was too important to the city, and that it would be cruel to take it from its habitat and expose it to the world's gaze. In 1905, Andrew Carnegie offered Long Beach one of his Carnegie public libraries, and the town had to make a decision--keep the beloved municipal whale or build a library.

In 1881, William Willmore approached Jotham Bixby on the Rancho Los Cerritos, asking him for land to form the "American Colony." The farming colony was to have a city, a 350-acre site extending from Magnolia to Alamitos Boulevard and from the ocean to 10th Street. In this city, which later become Long Beach, land was set aside for a park and a library. The park was Lincoln Park, where the civic center is today, and the site of the library was to be at Broadway & Pacific.

In 1884, Willmore could not pay his debt to Jotham Bixby and he sold his holdings for one dollar to a Los Angeles real estate concern called Pomeroy & Mills. It is a sad story, for if Willmore had been able to hold out until 1885, when the second transcontinental railway was built, he would have succeeded. In 1885, a price war developed between the Santa Fe and Southern Pacific rail lines. The one-way fare that used to be $52.50 fell to $4.00 in March of 1886. The result was a tremendous real estate boom.

John Bixby, who owned the neighboring rancho to the east, Rancho Los Alamitos, saw what was happening in Long Beach. People flocked to California because of cheap fares and to purchase land. Bixby decided to subdivide his Rancho in 1886. He too created a city called Alamitos Townsite, and set aside land for a park and a library. The park was Alamitos Park, later named Bixby Park in his honor. The library land was on 3rd Street where the Alamitos Branch Library is today.

Alamitos remained a separate city until 1909 when it was annexed to Long Beach. But in 1905 the citizens of Alamitos stepped forward and said they would gladly accept the Carnegie gift if Long Beach could not make up its mind where to put the library. Part of the problem was that a few years earlier, in 1899, Long Beach built a combined City Hall-Library on the site Willmore had originally set aside for a library. City fathers did not want to rip down their fairly new city hall for Carnegie, so they turned their eyes towards another source of free land, Willmore's park, which housed the whale.

Whale in park, on proposed site of library, c1903 L.B.P.L.

The public was outraged that the whale should be moved. Why not put the library somewhere else in the city? Well, Carnegie's gift was not totally free. In order to prove that cities believed in the public library ideal, they were asked to contribute a portion of the building expense. Long Beach felt it could do that if it did not have to spend money to purchase any land. When the neighboring Alamitos Townsite stepped forward, eager to claim a Carnegie library, Long Beach folk decided on a compromise: the library would be built in Lincoln Park and the whale displayed in the basement. And there the whale remained until the city built the Sun Parlor at the end of the Pine Avenue Pier with the Municipal Whale the focal point of the entire structure.

What happened to the whale that by the 1950s had been named "Minnie the Municipal Whale" by the local press? When the Pine Avenue Pier was closed because of storm damage in the 1930s, the whale was moved to a site at the Colorado Lagoon. There Minnie lay, her noble history forgotten, until the pavilion in which she was housed became an eye sore. The bones were removed in the 1950s and buried away in a city garage near the airport.

In June 1960, three Lakewood boys made a big discovery in a barley field near their homes--a mysterious cache of bones. Was it an elephant cemetery? They found ribs measuring 7 1/2 feet. They also found a vertebra that would do justice to any dinosaur. The lads carefully transported their precious cargo of bones to their school teacher, who was unsuccessful in identifying them. He did note, however, that the bones appeared to have holes bored through them and that small numbers could be observed on the monstrous vertebra.

The mystery was solved when the Long Beach Recreation Department identified the bones as parts of "Minnie the Whale," the largest and most

Dedication of library, 1908 L.B.P.L.

publicized mammal in the history of Long Beach. Recreation officials said that intruders had removed parts of the whale skeleton, but no one suspected the theft until they read about the large bone discovery in the paper. After finding the warehouse door standing open, the Recreation Department sent a crew to the homes of the three boys where most of the cache was stored. Had the boys stolen the bones and then made a publicity stunt out of it, or had the Recreation Department decided to get rid of the space-taking specimen and buried it one dark night?

In 1967, a few friends who remembered Minnie tried unsuccessfully to have her skeleton displayed next to Long Beach's newest tourist behemoth, the Queen Mary, to no avail. In 1974, her bones were donated to the Los Angeles County Museum of Natural History where they were disassembled and placed in the research collection. Today, only dispersed pieces of Minnie remain, but hopefully the memory of the important role she played in the early history of Long Beach will live on.

Captain Loop and "Sky Whaling"

Captain John Davenport Loop was definitely one of Long Beach's most interesting characters. On his whaling ship, the *Camiguin*, Loop took visitors on a not-soon-to-be-forgotten adventure. His fame spread across the nation and fishermen who wanted to be whalers came from far and wide just to go on a big game hunt with the notorious captain.

The *Camiguin* was equipped with an eight-bore Pierce shoulder gun which would fire bombs or lances at the mammal. A typical excursion, during which Loop landed a thirty-five-foot California Gray whale, was reported in the *Long Beach Press* on February 8, 1911. The newspaper stated there was great excitement when the bomb fired from the *Camiguin* struck the whale in the lungs. Although the whale lay stunned for a few seconds, it was far from dead. As it began to move around, one of the crew sent a harpoon with a 150-foot line into its back. The Gray raced away, but Captain Loop caught up with him and shot the animal in the head. The whale charged the boat, and at the last moment dived and headed under the craft. Another chase ensued and a third shot, fired into the lungs, finally brought the whale down.

WHALE

WHALE WHALE

Big California Gray Whale, captured by crew of 'Camiguin' now on exhibition at Municipal Docks. You must come soon. Thousands have seen it. Exhibition daily at 9 a. m. Admission 25c. Exhibited on barge giving full view of entire whale.

WHALE

L.B. Press 1/11/1913

Captain Loop regularly towed the whales he killed to his barge by the municipal pier. Here he would put his latest trophies on public display.

Admission was only twenty-five cents, but visitors had to come quickly if they wanted to view these wonders of the sea, which would only be there for a limited time. There was a problem with the foul smell of the decaying whale. However, Captain Loop made sure that the visitors toured the site from upwind of the barge so that the odor would be hardly noticeable. The smell was not so pleasant, however, for those living downwind from the rotting carcass. A week was all locals could stand before city officials ordered the whale remains towed out to sea or cut up for fertilizer. Loop's attraction did draw visitors to the area, a single whale could lure 2,500 people on a weekend.

Capt. Loop on whale, 1925 H.S.L.B.

Besides outfitting his barge for sightseers, Loop also had it designed to refine whale oil and manufacture fertilizer. The captain's dream was to revive the sluggish whaling industry which had prospered for many years, and nearly died out when the discovery of other oils threatened the whale-oil market. The California Gray whale, for instance, yielded about sixty barrels of raw oil called "mull." The grade of oil from the Gray was far inferior to that found in the Sperm whale, but it could still be used for lubricating purposes and for the manufacture of soap. In addition, Loop felt that whales made a splendid fertilizer and that the bones, when ground up, could be used for various purposes such as feed for animals. Loop, always efficient at handling money, realized it was far more economical to process the whale carcasses on his barge rather than sending them to a refining plant in Los Angeles.

In making fertilizer, Loop cut the whale carcass into pieces that were then cooked. Once softened, the flesh was ground up and pressed to get out the grease. After this, the ground flesh was pressed into bales, somewhat similar to bales of hay. These bales were then sent to local orange groves to be used as fertilizer. Captain Loop estimated the profits from a normal sized whale to be $1,000, after all expenses had been paid. His invention, the whale bomb, kept the overhead down. Firing bombs at whales was much more efficient than harpooning, or shooting them with regular rifles.

Though his patented whale bomb made whaling a much more efficient operation, Loop still had one major problem--how to keep the carcasses afloat until he reached shore. To solve this dilemma, Southern California's foremost whaler patented a gas lance for the capture of the sea mammals. Loop realized that times were changing. Since he had started his sea career, airplanes and dirigibles had come into vogue. These air machines, Loop felt, were destined to become the modern method of hunting whales.

John Loop's invention, a lance eleven feet long in the form of a cylindrical pipe, was designed to keep the carcasses afloat. The lance's penetrating end, four-sided and sharp, when dropped from the sky was fashioned to penetrate the whale's blubber without difficulty, if everything went according to plan. In addition, the lance carried three pounds of liquid carbon dioxide in a specially designed receptacle. The moment the lance penetrated the whale's body, the gas was released, keeping the whale afloat.

Captain Loop tested his lance, which he called a "blow devil" in August 1921 when he tried to hit a sixty-foot whale from a Navy blimp. Unfortunately, his aim was off. He brought the blimp down to within forty-feet of the surface and tried using his familiar whale bomb. This too failed to bring down the whale, which escaped and dived so deep that it was impossible to see the creature from the aircraft.

Loop was not a man to give up easily. It took him some time to convince the Navy to loan him a blimp for his research. A "smooth talker," Loop secured permission from the Secretary of the Navy, stressing the weapon potential of his novel device. In the August 19, 1921 issue of the *Daily Telegram* Loop reported on his adventure:

> To acquire proficiency in hurling my "blow devil" lance it will necessitate practice and lots of it. From the beginning of the development of aviation it has been proved that to attain skill in hitting a target beneath the airplane extensive practice is required. I believe with further experimentation the "blow devil" will answer the purpose for which it is designed. [1]

Loop believed that hunting whales from the air was destined to become a regular practice. By July 1922, his prediction proved true. The stunt of "aero whale hunting" was the favorite pastime of United States troops stationed in the Zulu Archipelago.

Always an innovator, Loop came up with other ideas for using whales. In 1916, after five years of research, he perfected a way to embalm any whale he captured. The captain still used the smaller ones for fertilizer, but with his new technique he could preserve the really big catches indefinitely, and they would be odor free. That same year, Loop and his crew worked out the details of a whale-meat preservation system. When he caught a beast not large enough for exhibition, Loop cut a few choice tons of "porterhouse." While still at sea, he treated the slices to his preservatives and once ashore sold it to the fish vendors on Pine Avenue or to local tuna packing plants. He said that those fortunate to have received samples of the meat agreed it was similar to beef, venison and buffalo, except for a peculiarly gamey flavor.

Whales were not the only sea creatures that interested Captain Loop. In the midst of World War I, the patriotic Loop came up with a process that substituted porpoise hide for rubber. Due to the short supply of rubber during the war, Loop invented a process for curing and toughening porpoise hide as a substitute for rubber. Originally, he tried whale hides, but his research proved that porpoise skin was much better. Fortunately, for porpoises the War ended the next year and their hides were saved from Captain Loop.

Though he came from a wealthy family and did not need the money, most of Loop's ventures proved profitable. Besides selling whales for fertilizer, he convinced the U.S. Food Administration to market whale meat during World War I. Following the War, he continued to make newspaper headlines throughout the United States with his novel ideas. In 1919, Loop returned from Mexico with a large receptacle full of whale's milk. Newspapers reported that a whale dairy "might be established" at Catalina Island. Later, Arthur De Eli of Omaha, Nebraska sent Loop an order for the lacteal fluid, but only if the price was not too high and it could be guaranteed to reach Omaha in good condition. Loop, however, was not certain how he would capture a large school of whales, keep them in captivity and go about milking them on a daily basis.

Motion picture companies frequently used Loop when they wanted whale-hunting scenes. On a cruise to Catalina Island with Buster Keaton, Loop was knocked overboard when a harpoon gun, which he was trying to operate, broke loose from its fastenings. The gun went overboard and Loop was badly cut. All this was caught by two cameramen who incorporated the accident into the film.

Captain J.D. Loop was not Long Beach's only inventor. The area around Alamitos Bay and Naples seemed to lure innovative individuals. In fact, in the days before World War I when anyone mentioned Alamitos Bay, one immediately thought of science-minded people. For instance, a motorist passing through Naples might observe one of the Trumble one-man submarines slipping from the moorings of a scow. A visitor might also see one of the Blake brothers stepping off a dock in his latest pair of water shoes, attempting to walk-on-water as in biblical times. There was an industry trying to manufacture a leather substitute from skins of sharks and other shallow water fish. Others were working on a new style motor, which gathered power from water friction, and a wave motor generator.

But none of the other Long Beach inventors were as eccentric as Captain Loop, who could often be found performing acrobatic stunts on his trampoline. When he was not whale hunting, this son of an Episcopal clergyman was cultivating a profitable career in real estate with investments around Pomona.

Whaling Today

By the end of the 20th century, there was an international moratorium against whale hunting.. Japan was the only country exempted from the 1986 International Whaling Commission ruling, restricted to hunting whales in its local waters for research purposes only. Norway ignored the regulations altogether.

Captain Loop was right about the delicious taste of whale meat. In 1998, an international black market in whale flesh was flourishing in Japan and South Korea. Japan claimed the meat they sold came from whales captured for research. Yet, a piece of whale meat obtained from a Japanese fish market was found to be from a variety of humpback whale found only in Mexican coastal waters. Investigators also found southern hemisphere Sei whale, Bryde's whale, North Pacific minke, fin and blue whale meat on sale in Japanese markets, all supposedly protected from hunting.

Canada joined the ranks of nations defying the moratorium on whale hunting when they gave the Inuit communities of the eastern Arctic permission to kill whales. On April 1, 1999 a 733,000 square-mile region inhabited by 25,000 people, mostly Inuit, broke away from the Northwest Territories and became a semiautonomous homeland. The people of the Baffin Island settlement, once a renowned whaling station, were anxious to revive a tribal tradition that was denied them for over fifty years. As part of the deal that created the new territory, the Inuit won the right to resume hunting for bowhead whales, an endangered species.

The first such hunt, near the mouth of Hudson Bay in 1996, was a bloody disaster that humiliated the Inuit. A team of hunters chased down a bowhead using high-tech sonar gear, then riddled it with bullets. But the carcass sank, washing ashore several days later to rot. In 1998, the tribe was more successful. Hunters, armed with an exploding harpoon, made a clean and swift kill.

The International Whaling Commission condemned the hunt and implored Canada to ban it. The Bowhead whales in the eastern Arctic were hunted to near extinction. Only 700 survive around the Baffin Island settlement. Environmentalists say that the whale population can not withstand any level of hunting, even though the Inuits are planning on only killing one whale every two years.

Whales off Long Beach, 1980s L.B.P.L.

The California Department of Fish and Game reported that most of the animals in our coastal area are really sea lions, with an occasional harbor seal thrown in. Sometimes people have a hard time telling them apart. Supposedly, it is quite easy to distinguish a sea lion from a seal. Sea lions have external ears and can fold their hind flippers under them. They are actually "California" sea lions, and their nearest kin, the Stellar sea lions, hang out around the North Pacific. Harbor seals appear "spotted" when they dry out and are also more "sausage" like in appearance. To early journalists, however, the harbor seal and California sea lion were simply "seals."

Both creatures are playful and often join swimmers in surfing waves and are not shy about pestering fishermen for handouts. They can be both entertaining and annoying, as the following stories will demonstrate.

Lassoing Seals

In the 1890s, capturing seals was a unique and little known industry in the great sea caves of Santa Cruz Island off the Santa Barbara Channel. Various seafarers made their living gathering seals and sending them to New York for distribution to various aquariums and circuses in the East. A few of the captives were even sent across the Atlantic to Germany.   In July 1899, the *Los Angeles Times* told the story of lassoing seals in the caverns of Santa Cruz Island, giving us a rare look at this novel enterprise.

First, the hunting party was lowered into rowboats and each member given a long rope for lassoing seals. They then headed towards the caves, which were literally alive with huge, brown-black figures that looked like the rocks themselves. As the boat approached, and the seals spotted the hunting party, the air filled with loud barks and roars which continued the entire time the men were in seal territory.

Despite the unfriendly welcome, the rowers passed through the entrance of a cave and beached the boats. As quickly as possible, they raised their lariats to try to catch as many seals as they could before the herd dispersed.   Once an animal was captured, the intrepid hunters tackled the exciting and dangerous feat of tying the flippers.   Using a short rope, one man approached the seal while the others pulled hard on the rope already over the snapping creature's head.   Once this exhausting work was done, all of the men dragged the seal to the water. At the shore, the men would get into their boats and tow the angry animal to an open space on the beach where crates were waiting.

When the captured beast was in the crate, the ropes were loosened from the seal's body and he began his fearful struggle to get free. Tying a stout rope to the container, the hunters then towed it to a kelp bed a short distance from the shore. Here the men wove long strands of seaweed around the seal's prison to keep it secure. Once done, they returned to the caves for a new catch, leaving the poor captive to reflect on his fate. Keeping track of the tide was vital. It was important that the seal trappers move their catch to the mother ship before the tide got too high. If they did not, they might drown the seals destined for the East and Europe.

A few seals did manage to evade the men and wreak revenge by biting the hunters trying to capture them. It was dangerous and exhausting work. There had to be an easier way to harvest seals, such as a seal farm.

Seals in Alamitos Bay, c1920 First American Title Insurance Co.

Seals have always loved Alamitos Bay, an inlet that separates Long Beach from neighboring Seal Beach. In 1915, Captain Owen Hugdan, a well-known authority on seals and their habits, recognized this fact and decided that the bay was a perfect place to start a seal farm. Hugdan's plan was to make his farm the foundation of an international supply station for educated seals and sea lions. Vaudeville shows and circuses were clamoring for these entertaining creatures. The market was there, why not cut down the costly expense of capturing them by raising them in a habitat they already loved?

One thing Hugdan did not take into consideration was that seals were by nature wild sea animals, and they did not take well to breeding in captivity. Despite all of his efforts to make the seals feel at home, Captain Hugdan was forced to abandon his idea of a seal farm when the creatures would not cooperate by procreating.

The Curse of Lake Elsinore

In 1925, Long Beach faced a dilemma. What was the city to do with the colony of seals residing in Alamitos Bay, which had local fishermen so upset? If Captain Hugdan had still been around, he may have persuaded the city to turn the seals over to him, but he moved from the area and no one else shared his vision of a seal farm. The problem for the fishermen was that a seal with a normal appetite consumed eight to ten pounds of fish daily. According to angry anglers, this was only a fraction of the fish the seals killed each day. To make matters worse, seals also destroyed fishing nets. A fight was brewing, not only between the fishermen and the seals, but between Long Beach and its neighbor across the bay--Seal Beach.

In 1913, enterprising real estate developers, who were also the city fathers of Bay City, decided to promote the playful marine creatures that lived on the sand spit at the mouth of Alamitos Bay. They did this by changing the name of their town to Seal Beach. What ensued was one of the most extensive real estate promotion schemes to date. For over a year, readers of area newspapers were treated to

Promotional ad for Seal Beach - *LB Press* 8/29/1913

a daily dose of ads showing cute seals. Tourists, who would hopefully buy Seal Beach real estate, flocked to the seaside resort to watch the intriguing creatures. Conscious that the success of selling land rested on promoting the seals, Seal Beach officials quickly passed an ordinance giving the seals the city's protection against irate fishermen.

On March 21, 1925, Long Beach Recreation Superintendent Squire DuRee announced a novel idea--move any seals that ventured to the Long Beach side of the bay to Lake Elsinore. DuRee felt that the Riverside County lake would be an ideal spot because it was stocked with carp, which humans do not like to eat, but would make fine feed for the seals. With the seals out of the way, the State could stock Alamitos Bay with striped bass and other edible fish, making it one of the greatest fishing spots in the world. DuRee was certain that yellowtail, barracuda, sea trout, halibut, smelt and whitefish would throng to the sheltered waters of the bay. DuRee neglected to give a cost estimate or plan on how one would move the fifty to seventy seals currently in Alamitos Bay, or the several hundred that migrated there each April. He also failed to take into account the seal's preference for salt water and the "Curse of Tondo" that surrounded Lake Elsinore.

The legend of the curse went back to the time of the Soboba Indians, a tribe who lived on the lakeshore. Tondo, the tribal chief, had a lovely daughter named Morning Star who fell in love with Palo, a member of the enemy Palas tribe. When Tondo discovered the two were lovers, his rage exploded. The couple, knowing they could not escape Tondo's wrath, walked hand-in-hand into the depths of the lake followed by a group of orphan children whom Morning Star befriended. As they walked to their death, Tondo stood on the shore and uttered his curse. From that moment, old-timers claimed strange things began to happen to the lake. Three hundred springs of boiling mud appeared soon afterward, and the valley reeked with sulfur. Mysterious lights were said to dance over the water, boats capsized for no apparent reason, and strong swimmers dived into the lake never to return. In 1833, and again in 1864, all the fish in the lake floated to the surface, dead. In 1840, hordes of gnats made life miserable for valley residents, and in 1951, the lake dried up.

Who would want to subject the friendly seals of Alamitos Bay to the curse of Lake Elsinore? What dire events might befall them? Would they end up dead like the fish? Maybe they would mutate into a different species. The seals' appearance would certainly have added to the strangeness of the lake and helped to perpetuate the legend.

A more practical solution to the seal problem surfaced a few days later when Recreation Park Superintendent Frank H. Downs suggested enclosing the seals in the lagoons of Recreation Park. "Go to the Bronx Park in New York or to Golden Gate Park in San Francisco and you will see that more people are gathered around the seals than around any other object of interest," Downs told the *Press Telegram*. He believed that the seals would prove to be one of the greatest tourist draws to the park.

While Long Beach was debating, Seal Beach was acting. They introduced a bill in the California legislature officially protecting the seals, and despite pressure against the legislation from Long Beach, succeeded in making it law. The seals would be secure in Alamitos Bay until the 1950s, when the creation of the Alamitos Bay yacht harbor drove most of them away.

Seal Beach pier & the scintillator, 1920's First American Title Insurance Co.

Pet Seals

If one happened to live around the shores of Alamitos Bay up through the 1950s, the likelihood of being adopted by a seal was good. As far back as the turn of the century, newspapers were talking about the special relationship between humans and the silky, black mammal. In 1906, the *Daily Telegram* related the tale of how young Will Graves caught a baby seal in his net while fishing. After keeping it a few days, Will lost interest in the little fellow. He ended up giving it to Mrs. A.E. Hall, who took it home to keep company with the other pets she had. The seal, "Jimmy," provided with a tub of water and plenty of fish, thrived well and grew at an amazing speed. In no time at all the young seal's weight went from sixty-five pounds to one hundred fifty-four pounds. Despite its size, it was gentle and intelligent and quickly learned manners and tricks. Jimmy was especially fond of Mrs. Hall and insisted that she scratch and pet him several times each day.

Word about Jimmy and the tricks he could do quickly spread. Hearing about the talented seal, animal buyers from Forepaugh & Sel's Brothers' circus came to see Jimmy. They were delighted with his intelligence and offered quite a sum of money for the personable seal. They said Jimmy was one of the few seals that could be educated, as shown by his long shapely head. A short stubby headed seal, they revealed, could not be trained. After much soul searching Mrs. Hall accepted their offer, saying that Jimmy was growing too big to be looked after. She also thought that Jimmy would have a fun time as a member of the circus.

Seals at Alamitos Bay, 1920s L.B.P.L.

By 1950, the animal control department in Long Beach frowned on people having pet seals. The animals belonged in the sea, the biologists said, not in a backyard pool. But what could be done if a seal would not go away? That was the dilemma Stuart Thomas and Gary Hollander of Belmont Shore faced in April 1950.

Sailing Alamitos Bay in Stuart's eight-foot sabot, the boys looked behind them and there was a baby seal, happily flipping along in the wake of the sailboat. The lads reached down and petted the two-foot seal. Encouraged by their friendliness, the young sea mammal struggled aboard and made himself at home, wagging his hindquarters at the two youths like a dog. The boys christened him "Joe." When they tied up the boat, Joe hopped onto the raft landing. That was when the seal's mother spotted him. She started bellowing in no uncertain seal-like terms for her wayward son to return home. Joe ignored her. Instead, he decided to stay with his new friends, allowing them to pick him up and carry him home. Stuart and Gary fed him warm milk and sardines, but Joe did not care for the canned fish.

Joe was still a baby, demanding constant attention and food. This was more than Stuart and Gary could deal with. They did not know what to do with their new friend so they called the Animal Shelter. The people there asked if the seal was injured. When told that he was not, they suggested the boys take Joe back home to the bay. Stuart and Gary complied. Joe, however, was not satisfied with the reception he received from his mother upon his arrival home. He decided to return for seconds on that warm milk. The boys took him back to the bay again, but Joe turned up for an early breakfast the following day. Animal Shelter workers told the boys to eliminate Joe's rations. They believed Joe's mother was amply equipped to provide her offspring with nourishment. If Joe got hungry enough, and could not get any chow elsewhere, chances were he would stay by his mother's side. Stuart and Gary had a hard time saying "no" to Joe. After all, they were boys too, and though they preferred sweets to fish, they could appreciate Joe's love of food. But resist they did, and eventually Joe went home to mom and a healthy, if not preferred, meal.

Mrs. Sam Ashbrook got a shock when she arrived at her Seaside Walk home one January evening in 1955. She reached down to pet her cat, Bootsie, but what she found instead was a fifty-pound seal. She was amazed, because her apartment was on the second floor and the seal had to have climbed twenty steps to get there. The Ashbrooks called their neighbors and, after they all pondered the problem, Mr. Ashbrook, who had seen many western movies, whipped off his belt. He formed a loop at one end and tried to lasso the animal. His aim was good, but he pulled the belt a little too tight and the seal started choking.

Seals at Alamitos Bay in the 1950s H.S.L.B.

Mr. Ashbrook felt terrible about harming such a friendly animal. He quickly loosened the belt and led the seal down the steps to the beach. The seal, however liked the Ashbrooks so much (despite the fact they put a noose around his neck), it came back and started to climb the stairs. Despite all their attempts, the Ashbrooks could not get the seal to leave. The police were called and they contacted the Animal Shelter who took the affable seal far out in Alamitos Bay. He never bothered the Ashbrooks again.

By April 1956, Long Beach built a marina in Alamitos Bay and had lost most of its seals. Not liking the noise and the commotion, the sea creatures moved away. Many would settle on the breakwater or the buoys that marked the channel. However, in 1998 they would again cause problems, not in Long Beach but in neighboring Newport Beach. In July 1988, the *Orange County Register* reported that gangs of sea lions had taken up residence in Newport Harbor. At first, the area residents were charmed by the sea lions, but they were not the politest of guests. According to various witnesses, the sea lions: flipped over a woman in a kayak who paddled into an area where they were feeding; ripped open commercial bait tanks with their sharp teeth; chased a cocker spaniel down a dock; bit a girl on the finger; jumped aboard a moving

Harbor Patrol boat and laid claim to several boats moored in the harbor forcing owners to move their vessels in an attempt to hide them from the homesteading sea lions.

There was no doubt the creatures were smart. At Newport Landing the sea lions figured out how to position themselves under bait tanks and blow bubbles up inside to scare the little fish. The tiny fellows would wriggle frantically out the sides of the tank into a waiting sea lion mouth. Marine mammal experts indicated El Niño was responsible for the influx of the sea lions. Warmer water temperatures diminished their food supply, driving them to the harbor in search of nourishment and rest. Officials hoped that as the water cooled and the sea lions' food supply improved they would leave.

The Marine Mammal Protection Act, passed in 1972, protects the California seal & sea lion population. By 1999 there were an estimated 175,000 of the mammals off the West Coast, an increase of more than five percent a year since the act was instituted. But there are problems. Seals and sea lions are killing off other endangered species. In February 1999, the Marine Fisheries Services asked for authority to eliminate sea lions and harbor seals feasting on endangered fish. Permission was also sought to destroy them at public beaches and marinas where they could endanger humans. In addition, the federal agency asked Congress to reinstate provisions of federal law that allowed commercial fishermen to kill seals and sea lions that destroyed their catch--something that Long Beach fishermen were striving for back in 1925.

N o story of sea creatures would be complete without a tale about sharks. Through the centuries there have been many stories of shark attacks, often fatal. However, of the 370 species of fish classified as sharks, only about a seventh are considered potentially dangerous to human beings. The most hazardous is the Great White shark, both because of its aggressiveness and its large size. The Mako shark is the most frequently involved in attacks on boats, most of which are unprovoked. Other large species that are dangerous are the Hammerhead shark, the Tiger shark and some of the Grey sharks. Though there are fewer than 100 shark attacks a year reported worldwide, many people still hold the mistaken belief that sharks attack any human being immediately. This is not true, and scientists are continuing to study why. Still, sharks are one of the most feared creatures of the sea, as the following stories show.

Who Ate Whom?

An intriguing shark tale was reported in the *Los Angeles Times* in 1883, aptly entitled "A Fish Story."

On August 27, 1883, a gentleman who lived in what was then known as Willmore City (now Long Beach), called the *Times* to recount the biggest fish story of the season. Since the man was considered honorable and reliable, and

Shark caught in Long Beach, April 1897 L.B.P.L.

not known to stretch the truth, the newspaper decided to print his story. The Willmore City resident (name not given) said that a shark between seven and nine feet long, was found on the beach about a mile west of the Willmore City Pavilion. The shark, which had its throat ripped open, had washed ashore, apparently killed by a swordfish. But the most interesting thing about the shark was that it had the tail of a barracuda sticking out of its mouth. The jaws of the dead shark were pried open and a two-foot long barracuda was extracted from the shark's mouth. This scenario presented quite a problem. The question in everyone's mind was: Did the shark try to swallow the barracuda, or did the barracuda try to swallow the shark, or did the swordfish try to swallow both of them? Though the topic was debated for many years, the ultimate fate of these fish remained shrouded in mystery.

Man-eaters

Man-eating sharks are not normally found in Southland waters, but one was reportedly captured here in February 1908. Fishing in his boat not far off of the Pine Avenue Pier in Long Beach, Clarence Owen hooked a young six-foot shark who had a good supply of sharp teeth. Fisherman Owens beat the shark over the head with an oar a dozen times before he dared to handle it or pull it into his boat. The corpse of the reported man-eater was put on public display for all to see.

A man-eating shark, striking at the end of a heavy tackle cast for swordfish, leaped out of the water and onto the deck of the yacht *Olita* in September 1912. Those aboard promptly clubbed the creature to death. There was much talk afterwards, not about the way in which it was killed, but as to its species. Was it truly a man-eating Great White shark? It was only thirty-eight inches long. Local taxidermist, W.R. Benbow, a recognized authority on animals, said that it truly was a member of the feared species.

Only once before in the history of the State had there been positive proof of full sized man-eating sharks inhabiting California waters, Benbow said. Twelve years earlier, in 1900, one was killed near San Francisco. In 1903, a rumor spread that a school of adult Great Whites had invaded the shores off Catalina. However, Great Whites seem to prefer colder waters, and the baby slain by the *Olita* party was probably a juvenile shark far from home.

It might not have been a Great White, but another shark scare occurred in 1913. Two police officers swimming 250 yards off Elm Avenue discovered a twelve-foot shark circling them. While the two men were swimming in the big waves in twenty feet of water, the shark floated on the surface sunning itself until the smell of the men reached its sensitive nostrils. The shark began to approach the swimmers, circling them, drawing nearer to its prey with each circuit. Almost paralyzed with fear, Will Rhodes and Harry Woods began their thrilling and record-breaking dash for land. The shark slowly followed them, staying within five feet of the two swimmers.

Shark captured off Long Beach in 1910 H.S.L.B.

The shark picked Woods out as his victim and came close to the swimmer's outstretched legs several times. Fortunately, the shark was frightened away by a splash on the part of the quick-witted policeman. While Woods kept the huge fish at bay, Rhodes swam to shore for help. Luckily, help was not needed. When Woods reached shallow water and the breaking waves, the shark left him.

In November 1955, Long Beach men hooked a 20 foot, 10 inch basking shark (which looked like a baby whale), fifty yards off the beach. Before it was brought in, the huge fish--estimated to weigh 2,500 pounds--towed a thirty-six foot water taxi more than an hour as the shark battled for freedom. While the hunt was on, its mate basked a scant twenty feet off shore, sunning its back in the shallows. The State Fish and Game Commission reported that the basking shark was uncommon south of the Santa Barbara Channel, but known to come into local waters. Often, they grow to forty-five feet, and many yarns about sea serpents are believed to have originated from mariners seeing these beasts. They feed on small sea organisms and are harmless to man. However, one could not convince any of the spectators witnessing the capture of this shark in 1955 of that fact. The creature was huge, and believed to be the biggest fish ever landed in Long Beach.

The Great Shark Scare of 1959

In June 1959, the water temperature off Southern California was six degrees warmer than usual. There was also an increase in reported shark attacks, with two people killed by sharks in La Jolla and San Francisco waters. Had man-eating sharks been attracted here because of the warmer water? Was there any correlation between the water temperature and the shark attacks, or was the pandemonium on Southland beaches only a result of mass hysteria?

Dr. Carl Hubbs, a Scripps marine biologist, told newspaper reporters there were several varieties of killer sharks that lurked in Southern California waters. First there was the "Requiem," a family that included the Blue, Tiger, Gray and Brown sharks. Scientists believed that some kind of Requiem killed the La Jolla skin-diver, though a Great White shark was first blamed. Requiems seemed to love the shark repellent tried by the Navy, and a Blue Requiem left shark toothmarks in a lifejacket after a fishing boat went down off Hermosa Beach in 1952. Some coastal lifeguards doubted that sharks were the culprits in the June 1959 La Jolla attack. Many thought the Orca or "Killer Whale," that often ventured into swimming areas and could be vicious, was the real cause of all the trouble.

Another variety of shark was the Great White, the man-eater that attacked and killed a swimmer in San Francisco and a swimmer near Pacific Grove in 1952. The good news, however, was that killer Great White sharks preferred cold temperatures and were not common in Southern California waters. If anything, the warmer water temperature experienced by the Southland in 1959 would have driven the Great White to colder waters further north.

"Hammerheads" are a type of shark that can be found locally. Though Hubbs once saw a Hammerhead knock a sea lion off a rock in one pass, I have found no recorded incidents of Hammerhead attacks on humans in California. However, they are known as man-eaters elsewhere in the world.

In the summer of 1959, Long Beach beaches were still crowded, but no one was venturing into the water farther than waist deep. Swimmers were advised to remain close to shore when a shark was sighted about a hundred feet off the end of Cherry Avenue on Sunday, June 21st. Local lifeguards patrolled in surfboats with .30-.30 rifles, and a Long Beach guard killed a shark while on the ocean front watch that day.

Huntington Beach residents reported that an eighteen-foot White shark was cruising the pier. This was especially terrifying for beach goers, who remembered the shark attack and death of a skin diver at La Jolla a few days earlier. Some speculated the undersea killer was attracted to the Huntington Beach pier by the blood and entrails thrown into the water by fishermen. However, Huntington Beach lifeguards, checking out the sighting, found nothing more than a clump of seaweed and a piece of driftwood.

Public hysteria increased when the watch of a missing Compton fisherman was discovered in the stomach of a shark. Edwin Gehle disappeared with his thirty-four-foot boat on June 4th. He was last seen aboard the *Helen G.* somewhere between Santa Barbara and Santa Catalina. The Coast Guard found no trace of either the man or his ship, but his watch was found on June 23rd. Gehle's watch was identified by his wife. The badly deteriorated timepiece was found in the stomach of a 750-pound shark caught about eleven miles off the isthmus of Catalina. The shark put up a good ninety-minute fight, but once the fishermen got it near their boat they shot the battling giant four times with a .30-.30 rifle. Authorities ruled out the possibility that the watch belonged to Robert Pamperin, killed June 14th by a shark at La Jolla, or Alfred Kogler, killed by a Great White at San Francisco on May 8th 1959.

Alarmed by the latest shark story, Long Beach City Councilmen directed the City Manager, Sam Vickers, to organize the 112-man lifeguard force for immediate protection. They also requested the City Manager seek help from all of the armed forces which normally operated planes, helicopters or boats in the offshore area. Vickers reported it was too late in the season to put up shark nets, but two lifeguard boats armed with harpoons were already on constant patrol. In addition, swimmers were warned not to venture beyond 150 yards from shore. The Mayor, Raymond Keeler, believed that two boats patrolling five miles of beach were not enough to cope with sharks that could travel fifty to sixty miles per hour.

Members of the Long Beach Civil Air Patrol immediately donated their services, organizing a "shark watch" along local beaches. The main purpose of the watch was to assure swimmers that all was safe, but the planes were also equipped with yellow smoke flares which could be dropped if a shark was sighted close to swimming areas.

Despite the shark scare, Mexican swimmer, Ramon Briseno Ocana, continued his attempt to set a new San Pedro Channel swim record. Starting his crossing of the twenty-one-mile channel at Marineland on the Palos Verdes peninsula, Ocana was only 5 1/2 miles from Catalina when he was surrounded by a pack of fifty Blue sharks. The Mexican accountant swam underwater to his escort boat while fifteen riflemen poured a volley of shots into the sharks. None of the sharks were killed. Ocana had enough though, stating he was giving up all professional swimming activities.

Dr. Nelson Mathison told reporters that the channel between the mainland and Catalina had been full of sharks for centuries. It was not uncommon for sharks to regularly follow any channel swimmer. According to Mathison, once it turned dark one could see the fluorescent wakes in the water left by sharks. Night was supposed to be the time they preferred to attack, but Mathison indicated that no one had ever been bothered by a shark on a channel swim before Ocana.

Robert Retherford, president of the California Council of Diving Clubs, told reporters there were fifty-six shark attacks in United States' waters between 1907 and 1959. Ten were fatal. Eleven of the attacks were in California and three of these resulted in death. Only one victim was a diver. Retherford reported that most of the so-called shark-fin sightings offshore were the fins of porpoises, ocean sunfish or sea lions floating in their characteristic pose with one fin elevated. He pointed out that fishermen always caught sharks in the channel between the mainland and the offshore islands. Usually they cut the shark up and threw it away. Now, with the 1959 shark scare, they would drag it back to shore and get their pictures in the newspapers.

Long Beach lifeguard captain Roy J. Miller refused to be taken in by all the shark hype. He stated there were always a few sharks offshore, and the danger of these fish was exaggerated. Miller could only smile when, in July, the fisherman who reported finding lost seaman Gehle's watch in a shark's stomach came forward and said that it was all a hoax to win a $200 bet.

Though 1959 was one of the hottest years on record, with little rainfall and air conditioning a common luxury of the future, few would venture far into the sea to cool off. Stories of shark sightings were frequent, and most Southern Californians preferred the sweltering heat to a possible encounter with one of the denizens of the deep.

L ife at sea could be dangerous, as Charles Barden, a Long Beach bookkeeper, found out in 1916. Barden and his friend, Fred Myers, set out on a fishing vacation in April 1916. However, their two-week holiday turned into six months of hell. Two shipwrecks, fever and forced enlistment in the Australian Army were only part of the tragedy, for Barden also had to watch his friend die.

A week into the trip the boat's engine broke down. The two men drifted for days, delirious from the sun and lack of food. At last, their craft ended up on a rocky island. For days they remained marooned there, still feverish. Believing their prayers answered, the *Manunut*, a boat bound for Auckland, New Zealand rescued them. Unfortunately, this vessel also floundered and went down off the island of Mouca near New Caledonia. The crew, including Barden and Myers, were picked up a few days later by a French ship headed for Sydney, Australia.

While in Sydney, Meyer's fever worsened and he died. Barden was now alone and desperate to return home to his family. Barden learned he could not leave Australia without a passport, and the only way to get one was to join the Army. After a month of service Barden's commanding officer observed Barden could not close his left hand because of a previous injury. This, coupled with the American consul's assistance, was enough to get the Long Beach bookkeeper a discharge and the proper papers to return home. Despite his advanced age of thirty-five, Barden managed to get a job as a cabin boy on the next available ship sailing for the West Coast. He returned home to an astonished family who had given him up for dead.

"She" Adventure

It was a monstrous and scandalous act, undoubtedly caused by reading too many romance and adventure novels. Margaret Scott cast aside her woman's clothing, cut her hair, and took on the guise of a man. Margaret become a sailor. Early twentieth century ideals defined women as delicate creatures who needed the protection of a man. The position of women in society centered around the idea of home and family with a woman's primary role as wife and mother. It may be difficult for women of today, who enjoy more equality with men, to envision the strict rules and regulations that controlled a woman's role at the turn of the century. A woman was expected to get married and have a family. Margaret Scott, however, wanted more. She wanted the adventurous life of a sailor. Even though life at sea held its dangers, Margaret Scott decided she would take her chances.

Bluff in Long Beach where Margaret Scott slept in 1905 H.S.L.B.

Margaret, the sailor, landed in Long Beach in September 1905. While waiting to sign on with a vessel sailing further afield, she took on odd jobs, sleeping in a cave under the bluff at Alamitos Beach. It was Long Beach police officer Folsom who first noticed Margaret, and became suspicious because of her good looks and mannerisms. Though she cut her hair short, and continued to dress in a sailor's outfit, there was just something about her that bothered Officer Folsom. He finally questioned some of the sailors who were on the last ship with Margaret. In doing so, Folsom learned that he was a she. Margaret did not hide her gender from her shipmates, but the captain who hired her did not know her true identity.

In talking with other sailors, the policeman learned that Margaret acted like a boy (though she was reserved and not inclined to be tough or rowdy), and constantly talked to her shipmates about her desire to be a man and go to sea. Hearing the truth, Folsom decided he had to arrest Margaret for her own protection. He took the girl who wanted to be a boy home with him and locked her up in the front parlor until the following morning when he could see what could be done.

Once rested, Margaret told her story. She stated it began in the summer of 1905 when she visited Anacapa Island off Santa Barbara with family friends. While there, she adopted the custom of some of the women--wearing male attire when making boat trips. Trousers were less cumbersome and more practical than huge skirts for traveling and fishing. One day, while sailing to Santa Barbara, she lost her own clothing overboard. When she reached the shore, she had only her suit of boy's clothes.

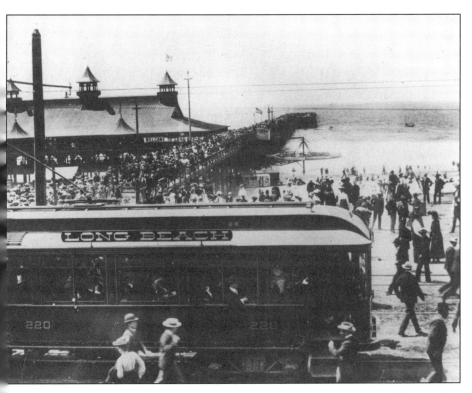

Margaret, the female sailor was put on the Red Car and sent home, photo c.1921 L.B.P.L.

This was when the story became questionable. Margaret said she had no money to buy clothes. She decided to continue wearing the male attire she had on until she could earn enough cash to make the change to women's garb. One has to wonder why she did not ask the family she was traveling with for a loan of clothing or money, or why she did not contact her family. In any case, in looking for work she ran across the owner of a small fishing boat, who hired her (thinking she was a he). Margaret began to enjoy the life and freedom of being a sailor.

Taken before Justice Brayton, Margaret talked freely, saying that she loved the ocean and had been reading sea adventure stories for several years. When the judge told her of the dangers that menaced young girls who acted as she did, Margaret replied that she was not afraid of any man and was able to take care of herself. She was fond of adventure and told the judge she wanted to be a boy because skirts interfered with her freedom of movement and action. While Brayton lectured her on her folly, she listened with a dainty shrug of the shoulders and kept up a constant low and musical whistling.

Finally, Margaret took the judge's advice and called her father in Santa Monica. Mr. Scott told officers to turn her loose and send her home, but he refused to pay the expenses for an officer to bring her directly to him. After another strong fatherly lecture, Margaret was taken to the Pacific Electric depot and put on a car for home. But Margaret did not go home. She disappeared again, only to turn up months later in San Diego when she was arrested for vagrancy. Here she told officials that she had learned a valuable lesson--to keep the fact that she was a girl to herself. Word spread among the sailors about her true identity and no one would hire her. She was forced, at least for a time, to return to her father.

Margaret was not the only young lady determined to lead a man's life. In 1904, Bessie Barclay, the seventeen-year-old daughter of a Los Angeles attorney ran away from home, becoming a cabin boy aboard a ship. She, too, shed her confining skirts, cut her hair and adopted male clothing.

Her parents, not happy with her decision, alerted police and Bessie was eventually arrested and put in jail. Her mother could not understand why her daughter had acted in such a manner. Bessie was an attractive young lady and a talented musician. But Bessie said she did not want to lead a pampered life and desired to get out in the world and have adventures. She told her parents she would run away again. As a result, they decided to send her to the Reform School in Whittier. Maybe there they could make her behave.

PART 2

STRANGE SHIPS
&
BURIED TREASURE

Southern California offers virgin and potentially fruitful waters for treasure hunting. It's thought that as many as 30 Manila galleons making the run from Manila to Acapulco may have gone down between San Francisco and San Diego.

Michael Parrish *Treasure Hunters.* 1983

The most bizarre story I ever found in Long Beach's newspaper archives concerns the Lizard people. In January 1934, an intriguing article appeared in the *Press-Telegram.* An Indian legend and a radio x-ray were enough to start a group of men digging in the heart of Los Angeles for a lost underground city of the Lizard people.

G. Warren Shufelt, a geophysical mining engineer, together with Hopi Indian Little Chief Greenleaf, felt they had located one of three lost cities on the Pacific Coast dug by the Lizard people.

Looking for the Lizard people? 1930s L.B.P.L.

According to legend, 5,000 years ago a great firestorm came out of the Southwest, destroying all life in its path. The Lizard people dug the labyrinths to escape future conflagrations. One of their cities lay within a chain of hills forming the frog of a horse's hoof. Shufelt believed the description fit an area within a few blocks of Los Angeles City Hall.

Tradition had it that the lost city was dug with powerful chemicals. The tunnels began at the ocean and the tide, passing daily in and out of the lower portals, forced air into the upper passages, providing ventilation. Large rooms in the domes of hills housed hundreds of families, who stored their food against the coming of another fire. The Lizard people were highly advanced and developed a cement better than any now in use. They laid their city out in the shape of a lizard, its tail pointing to the southwest. The explorers believed that a shaft, drilled at least 300 feet, would lead them to a room of catacombs. Here they expected to find the records of the Lizard people, written on tablets of gold.

Though no one ever found the remains of the Lizard people, many interesting fossil discoveries were made at the Long Beach Brick company's clay pit at Seventh and Ximeno. The knee bone of a camel, a fossilized whale vertebra and other prehistoric specimens were unearthed in 1914.   J.J. Chamberlain, foreman of the brick company, was involved in several other fossil finds. One was a discovery near Los Angeles of an ancient ship keel and prow, buried away under countless ages of soil.

Chamberlain told reporters the vessel was crudely fastened together with wooden pins and, undoubtedly, belonged to a period before the Vikings sailed the North Sea. The brick yard foreman believed it was possibly the broken remnant of Noah's ark or the monument of man's first attempt to navigate the waters. Unfortunately, we only have Chamberlain's word for what he saw--the mystery craft crumbled away to dust when exposed to the air. Not even a picture was taken or record made of its dimensions, which Chamberlain said must have been fifty or sixty feet in length, when whole.

What was it? In 1983, James Moriarty III, Professor of History and Archaeology at the University of San Diego, and a specialist in ancient ships, told reporter Michael Parrish that he believed Chinese ships crossed to California and Mexico 2,000 years ago. Could Chamberlain's find have supported Moriarty's theory? Perhaps the ship was one of the canoes used by Native Americans to travel to Catalina? Was it, in fact, a Viking ship or perhaps the remains of a pirate vessel or Spanish galleon? Several possibilities will be explored in the section that follows.

J.J. Chamberlain believed the mysterious craft he discovered in Los Angeles in 1914 may have been a Viking ship. His theory may not be as far-fetched as it seems. Choral Pepper, in her book *Desert Lore of Southern California*, argued that Vikings were in the Southland. She related the tale of how the famous Long Beach earthquake of March 10, 1933 buried an ancient Viking ship in the desert:

Pepper wrote that in their spare time, Myrtle and Louis Botts, of the small mountain town of Julian, liked to come to the Anza Borrego desert area to camp and look for new species of plants. In March of 1933, while in the desert near the current Agua Caliente San Diego County Park, an old prospector arrived to fill up his water bags. He told the couple that far into a nearby canyon he had seen an old ship sticking right out of the side of a mountain. They thought the miner had been out in the sun too long and did not take his story seriously.

The following day, while out looking for possible new plant specimens, they saw the ship. Jutting out of a canyon wall, almost immediately overhead, was the forward portion of a large and very ancient vessel. A curved stem head swept up from its prow. Along both sides of the boat were circular marks in the wood, possibly left by shields that may at one time been attached. The craft was too high for the couple to see the interior, and the side of the canyon so precipitous and unstable that they decided not to climb. The pair studied the curious site for some time before carefully retracing their steps to camp so they could locate it again.

Hardly had they emerged from the canyon when the infamous Long Beach earthquake struck. Both Myrtle and Louis were thrown to the ground. After the terrible shaking subsided they gathered their scattered supplies and hurried home, but not before discovering that the spring which had been cold the night before was now hot.

Back home in Julian, Myrtle, the librarian in charge of the public library tried to identify the ship. Research seemed to indicate that it was an old Viking ship, yet she found it hard to believe that one would be in the California desert. Before reporting her discovery, she wanted to take some photos. Myrtle and her husband returned to Agua Caliente the following weekend.

Once again they hiked to the canyon where they had seen the craft, but the entrance to the canyon was gone. Half of the unstable mountainside had fallen into the canyon during the earthquake. They realized they had just gotten out of there in the nick of time or they too would have been buried under tons of earth.

Choral Pepper said that she met Myrtle Botts, now deceased, and that she struck her as a down-to-earth woman not given to fanciful illusions. Pepper remembered a Seri Indian song she came across when she was writing an article on Tiburon Island, in the Gulf of Mexico, that could shed some light on the matter. The song told of the arrival of the "Came From Afar Man." According to Seri legend, a huge boat containing several large men with yellow hair and a woman who wore her red hair braided down her back appeared at Tiburon Island. They remained at the island for a long time while the men went hunting. When they had sufficient meat they left the land of the Seri.

Existing Viking texts reveal that ancient Viking sea captains carried their wives when they went to sea. These manuscripts also lead us to believe that Vikings sailed to North America long before the Spanish. Could they have arrived at a time when ancient Lake Cahuilla filled the Salton Sink, to or above sea level with the Colorado River, providing a waterway link to the Sea of Cortez?

Reference to a Viking ship in the desert appeared in an article in the *Press Telegram* on April 21, 1929. It told of a trip by several Long Beach folk to the Salton Sea to look for the elusive vessel. Evidently, the legend had been around for some time, starting with an early prospector named Santiago Socia who returned home to Mexico City with one of the shields from the vessel.

An intriguing record turned up in Guadalajara, Mexico in the 1950s, reporting an official inquiry held by the Spanish court in 1574. A strange fleet of three large and five small vessels were sighted sailing north in the Gulf of California. Because they obviously were not of Spanish origin, the Crown ordered an investigation. Author Clive Cussler took the legend to form the basis for his adventure novel *Inca Gold*. In it, he saw the ships as Incan vessels escaping the destruction of their empire by the Spanish. They were traveling north with treasure and other valuables when they were beached in the now California desert.

Who knows which story to believe, if any. Finding the ship would be an archaeological treasure. Someday, perhaps, another earthquake will reopen the blocked canyon and again reveal the ancient vessel seen by the Botts. Those of us who live around Long Beach hope, at least, that it is not another Long Beach centered quake.

When J.J. Chamberlain discovered the ancient ship in fossilized strata in 1914, he thought it could have also been a remnant of Noah's Ark. Of course it was not, but there was another type of ark that would become part of Long Beach history.

In 1916, African-American minister, James E. Lewis began to build an ark. Receiving "divine guidance" from God, he was told to construct a 115 foot ship, sail it to the African nation of Liberia and spread the word of the Lord. On October 10, 1919, the vessel was launched. The ceremonies started with Lewis' wife Levinia breaking a bottle containing water and honey on the bow of the ship. As part of the religious ceremonies, a lamb, five chickens, seventeen dogs and three cats were assembled in the vessel as the ship started her slide toward the water. Then something happened. Within six feet of the Pacific, the boat broke in two. Undaunted by the unfortunate attempt, Reverend Lewis announced he would rebuild his ship and sail it to Liberia.

Try again he did. The ark was back in the news in January 1921. Lewis was busily building his second ark, which towered over J. Kohara's machine shop on Terminal Island. The ship was 125 feet long, 25 feet high with a beam of 35 feet. It was constructed of odd bits of wood, planks and other building material. Neighbor Kohara was not happy with the activity going on next door and he took Lewis to court. Kohara, arguing that the ship was on his property, obtained a judgment for $90 against Lewis in an ejection suit and later was granted a writ of possession of the land. A deputy sheriff was given the papers and told to remove the ark, but the ship was so unwieldy and so far from the water that the writ was returned as unserved. Kohara filed suit for abatement of a nuisance and sought $900 in damages. He claimed that the boat rested on his property and shut out the sunlight and air from his shop.

In winning his suit, local authorities empowered Kohara to destroy the ark and delay, for the time being, Reverend Lewis' voyage to the "promised land." Kohara and Lewis settled their differences, and the ark--a queer shaped hulk of wood and cement--survived. Long Beach's Noah energetically raised $18,000 to build the craft, which would house members of the congregation of the "Church of the Living God." Nautical experts said the ship would not float, and the Harbor Commission feared that the "Ark" would sink and clog up the harbor. Lewis finally obtained permission, and the vessel was moved to the water's edge. It refused to float. The evangelical minister then attempted to buy the ship *Angel*, but could not come up with enough cash.

J.E. Lewis was not one to give up. In December 1922, with the financial support of wealthy Los Angeles African American C.J. Darrough, Lewis announced he had formed, and become president of, the Liberian Transportation and the Living God Shipping Line. According to the clergyman, negotiations were underway for the purchase of the steamer Charles D.B. King, formerly the naval supply ship *Brutus*. Over 100 persons from all parts of the country would be on board when she sailed on February 3, 1923 for Liberia. Oscar Hudson, Liberian consul at San Francisco came to San Pedro on January 30, 1923 to confer with Lewis and give his official approval.

Did Lewis and his followers sail? Did they reach Liberia, the country settled by former African-American slaves? Unfortunately, no further news about the ark was reported, which leads one to believe they did not make their sailing date. On January 30th, they were still completing negotiations to purchase the Charles D.B. King. One hopes, however, that they succeeded in securing a suitable ship, that it reached its goal and that the Reverend Lewis was able to fulfill his dream of bringing his Christian ideals to the natives of Liberia.

For centuries Manila galleons, tall, heavily ornamented Spanish battleships, sailed off our coast. Perhaps one of them was the vessel uncovered by J.J. Chamberlain in 1914. The Manila galleons were the largest ships owned by Spain. They were seagoing monsters of 1,200 and even 2,000 tons, carrying up to 60 cannons and over a 1,000 people. Beginning in 1565, up to three ships loaded with riches from the Americas, sailed from Acapulco in March, landing in Manila by July. Once trading negotiations were complete, the same ships, filled with luxuries of the Orient, sailed back across the Pacific to Mexico, arriving around January. From Acapulco, the cargo was hauled overland by mule to Veracruz where other galleons took the riches across the Atlantic to Spain.

And riches there were. These Manila galleons were so heavily laden that at least one sank from overloading as it was leaving port in the Philippines. The cargo included exports from all over the Far East. Chinese products included rich silks and brocades, tea, gold, porcelain art treasures, carved wood furniture and fruits. From Japan there was lacquerware, porcelains and cutlery. Borneo and the South Seas islands supplied cocoa, ceramics, pearls and semiprecious stones. From Siam (Thailand) and Burma came spices, ivory, gold, jade and amber. India furnished gold, ivory, precious stones and perfumes. The Philippines shipped pearls and precious ornaments made by Chinese goldsmiths in Manila, and gold bullion.

On the return leg to Acapulco, the galleons rode the Japanese current that began in the Philippine Sea, took them past Japan and then to the land that would one day become California. The crew usually sighted land between Eureka and Mendocino, but because of the threat from pirates, the galleon captains were not allowed to drop anchor. Instead, they turned south at the sight of land, heading down the misty coastline toward New Spain (current day Mexico). Eventually, California was explored by the Spanish to locate safe harbors, should a Manila galleon need repairs after a tough Pacific crossing. Missions, and eventually towns, developed as a result of the Pacific trade.

These Spanish ships were not very seaworthy. Top heavy, with as many as four decks, their gun ports were so close to the water line that even a modest sea could sink a galleon if a gunner left a porthole open. They were also hard to maneuver, almost always overloaded and usually in need of repair.

Captains with no experience often bought their positions for a chance to bring back fortunes, leaving navigation and such trivialities to lesser officers. These treasure ships were run by the Spanish government, and strict rules were issued as to what they could or could not do. By royal decree, no other ship could tie up next to a galleon in port. There were prohibitions against the galleons sailing at night, and coded lights at harbor entrances warned of lurking buccaneers.

For 250 years, longer than the United States has been a nation, these heavily laden giants made their way across the sea from Manila to California, always on the lookout for pirates. Crews were especially apprehensive as they approached the galleon graveyard around the notorious pirate island of Santa Catalina.

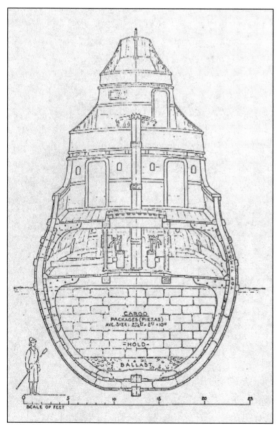

Inside of a Spanish galleon

Treasure hunter Dave Horner, conducted a statistical study of the ships making the Atlantic crossing to Spain from 1497 to 1612. He calculated that 12% of the galleons were shipwrecked and completely destroyed.

In the Caribbean, almost 2,000 Spanish treasure ships slipped beneath the waves. It is thought that between 1565 and 1825 at least thirty Manila galleons, making the run from Manila to Acapulco, sank between San Francisco and San Diego. There may be more, but until a thorough investigation is completed of the archives in Spain, we may never know.

Why do we never hear of any fantastic treasures found in our Pacific waters, like those found in the Caribbean? Though Southern California offers virgin and potentially fruitful waters for treasure hunting, the going is not easy. In the Caribbean, divers work in relatively shallow waters of forty-five feet or less. They simply remove the sand over the old wrecks. Here the water is much deeper, and the going much harder. Where are these Pacific wrecks? James Gibbs, in *Shipwrecks of the Pacific Coast*, provided a detailed chronology of all ships sunk off the Western United States up to 1962 and where they supposedly went down. Have some of them been found? Perhaps they have. However, treasure hunters (and finders) usually operate in secrecy to keep others away.

Offshore Spanish Wrecks

Off Catalina lies the *Santa Marta*, an early Manila galleon that went aground on Catalina Island in 1582. Before she broke up her crew and passengers escaped ashore. Some of her treasure was taken off immediately. John Potter, author of *The Treasure Diver's Guide*, believed that 200 tons of Far East treasures went down with her shattered hull. However, a Spanish salvage expedition sent from Acapulco the following year may have recovered some of the treasure.

The 230 ton *Nuestra Senora de Ayuda* struck a rock west of Santa Catalina Island and sank in 1641. Some of the crew members made their way safely ashore, but the merchandise and treasure she carried was not recovered. Potter believes it is there somewhere, strewn over patches of stone ballast on a shallow reef. Her nonperishable cargo would be worth over a $1,000,000 today.

The *San Sebastian* was heading toward Acapulco through the outer Santa Barbara Channel on January 7, 1754 when the English pirate George Compton attacked. The *San Sebastian's* captain tried to escape, but only succeeded in running his ship aground on a rock fang a short distance from Santa Catalina island. The galleon sank quickly. Twenty-one of her crew and passengers reached shore only to be killed by the pirates. Potter believes the broken ship lies off the west shore of Catalina in about 170 feet of water, undoubtedly buried deep under shifting sands.

Thomas Penfield, author of *A Guide to Treasure in California*, reported a Spanish frigate supposedly went down off the northwestern tip of Catalina

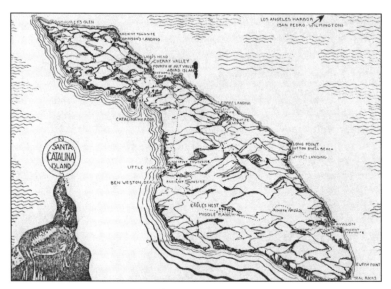

Map of Catalina Island, 1940s L.B.P.L.

with a cargo of treasure valued at $1,300,000. However, he questioned this claim because Spanish frigates were not used in the Pacific to escort treasure-laden galleons. They were used in the Atlantic to protect Spanish treasure fleets, but in order to give them more speed, their cargoes were kept as light as possible.

Potter wrote that a California forty-niner on his way to the gold fields, was looking down through forty feet of clear water near the southeastern tip of Catalina Island off Seal Rock when he spotted the outline of an old ship. Spanish explorer Sebastian Vizcano, landing on Catalina in 1602, wrote that the Indians there showed off Chinese silks that had washed ashore. They probably came from the *Santa Marta*.

The Channel Islands off Santa Barbara may also contain treasure. Anacapa Island is full of caves, the largest of which is said to have been used by early pirates as a hideout and base of operations. Tradition says the pirates left treasure buried on the island where it remains hidden to this day. There are stories of treasure buried by the Portuguese explorer, Cabrillo, and Sir Francis Drake, in the caves of San Nicholas Island. Also, an unidentified Spanish galleon is said to have gone down off San Nicholas in the 1730s. The vessel, according to unconfirmed accounts, was carrying $1,000,000 in Mexican gold.

Point Bennett, at the western end of San Miguel Island, is reportedly the final resting-place of several wrecked vessels, from Manila galleons to early twentieth century schooners. The problem, however, is that the reefs are treacherous and almost impossible to search. One alleged wreck may be easier to reach--it is supposedly buried in the sand hillocks on the south side of the island.

Oceanside Treasure

Other Spanish galleons lie off our shore, according to author John Potter. The *Trinidad*, the first Spanish ship to visit California, was sent up the coast from Mexico by Hernando Cortez to find the rumored Seven Cities of Cibola. Indians told of incredibly rich cities to the north, called the Seven Cities of Cibola, where entire streets were paved with gold. Cortez hoped to lead a band of soldiers to find this city, when orders from Mexico City stopped him. Instead of Cortez, the Viceroy selected Francisco Coronado to lead the expedition.

Embittered, Cortez chafed at the bit while Coronado, then De Soto, led unsuccessful attempts to find the fabled wealth. Then, in 1539 at his base in western Mexico, Cortez could restrain himself no longer. He decided to ignore the Viceroy's orders and plan his own search. Cortez felt that somewhere up the unexplored western coast of America, was a navigable waterway along which small ships could travel inland. He had three suitable ships at Acapulco: the *Santo Tomas*, the *Santa Agueda*, and the *Trinidad*. Early in 1539, he sent them north under the command of his trusted lieutenant, Francisco de Ulloa.

Ulloa was not as loyal as Cortez hoped. No sooner had the small fleet got underway than Ulloa scuttled the *Santo Tomas*, which carried a crew loyal only to Cortez. The two remaining ships sailed on, charting Lower California and its gulf, which they named the Sea of Cortez. When they reached the island of Ceros off Mexico, Ulloa packed the remaining men loyal to Cortez into the *Santa Agueda* and sent them back to Acapulco. With twenty-four loyal followers, he continued north in the thirty-five ton *Trinidad*.

According to Potter, nearly all of Ulloa's men were the errant sons of Spanish nobility. Because of misdeeds at home, were sent to the New World in disgrace. There was little hope of them ever returning to Spain, and they had all the money they possessed with them aboard the *Trinidad*.

Thomas Penfield reported a somewhat different story. He said that about $10,000,000 worth of gold packed in pitch-covered boxes, taken in Mexico to finance the trip, were stored in the hold. Both Potter and Penfield agreed that Ulloa put in at the mouth of the San Luis Rey River, by present day Oceanside, on June 30, 1540, hoping that he had found the inland passage.

Map of San Diego Co.

First, Ulloa and his crew decided to do some exploring on land, questioning the natives about the Seven Cities. All but three of the men went ashore, taking some of the wealth with them.

While staying with the friendly Indians, Ulloa and his men contracted scurvy and they all died. Too weak to return to the ship, they are said to have buried the treasure they carried near the Indian settlement. Supporting this incident is the fact that a mass grave was found inland from Oceanside in 1937. The skulls had no teeth nor roots, the mark of men who die of scurvy. Bits of armor, a few buttons and other artifacts of Spanish origin were found, strengthening the belief that these were the remains of Francisco de Ulloa and his crew. In the 1950s, Dr. Joseph J. Markey, an Oceanside physician and treasure hunter, reportedly found 2,000 coins minted before 1540 in the area around the Mission San Luis Rey.

One of the three men left aboard the *Trinidad* was the historian of the voyage, Pablo Salvador Hernandez. He left behind the records on which this story was based. After weeks of waiting for the return of Ulloa and his men, the three seamen gave them up for dead and decided to return to Mexico. Because they could not handle the *Trinidad* alone, they constructed a longboat and finally made their way back to New Spain. While they were building their new vessel, a storm struck in August of 1540. According to Potter, the unmanned caravel was torn loose from her moorings and blown down the California coast meeting her end somewhere off Point La Jolla.

Penfield, however, believed the ship may lie off the mouth of Loma Alta Creek and the 1600 block of Pacific Street in Oceanside because Spanish coins have washed ashore there. These coins, however, might have come from another Spanish ship, *Madre de Dios*, reportedly sunk off Carlsbad, about two miles south of Oceanside. There have been unconfirmed reports that $150,000 was recovered from this wreck.

The remains of another wreck were reported in 1956 when a skin diver announced that he found what appeared to be the hull of a galleon off Solano Beach in sixty feet of water. Scientists at the Scripps Institute of Oceanography were doubtful about his claim. They indicated there would be no remaining wood because woodborer worms would have made sawdust out of the vessel long ago.

One other shipwreck bears mention, the Spanish galleon *Santa Rosa*. This vessel sank in 1717 when she hit a shoal called Bishop Rock on the outer point of Cortez Bank, southwest of the Coronado Islands near San Diego. It too, reportedly awaits discovery.

Mission Treasures

In *A Guide to Treasure in California*, Thomas Penfield gives an extensive list of reported treasure sites in our state, including mission treasures.

The twenty-one California missions were started in 1769 with the founding of San Diego de Alcala in present day San Diego. The last, San Francisco Solano, was built in 1823 in the town of Sonoma. In 1810, New Spain broke away from the mother country and set itself up as the Republic of Mexico. The effects of this move on the California missions were far-reaching. Channels of authority became confused, the missions had to support themselves entirely and also supply the civilian and military settlers. Then, in 1833 came the ruling to secularize the missions.

Politicians believed the missions had fulfilled their function of civilizing the natives, and it was time for them to be replaced with another colonial institution, the pueblo. One by one, the California missions were secularized over the next sixteen years. The mission orchards, fields and buildings passed into private hands and the mission system collapsed. Throughout all of this, legends arose about mission gold and treasures. In reality, it is extremely doubtful that any of the California missions possessed much to bury or hide away. Yet the stories persist.

Penfield reported an early California legend in which a cart full of gold was buried in Santa Inez Canyon, not far from where Sunset Boulevard meets Pacific Coast Highway in Malibu. According to the story, in 1836 two priests, accompanied by a few Indians, were driving a cart heavily laden with gold from the San Fernando Mission to the harbor at San Pedro. At the mouth of Santa Inez Canyon, they were attacked by bandits. As the Indians fought off the attackers, the padres rolled the cart into a nearby marshy area where it sank out of sight. Neither the Mission fathers nor the Indians survived the attack, so one can only surmise the story came from the bandits. When Sunset Boulevard was put through to the coast, the marsh was filled in. Nothing was found. Does the treasure still exist?

Treasure may exist in San Diego's Old Town area, buried by the priests from the original mission. One version of the tale tells of the padres digging a tunnel from the mission to the bottom of a nearby canyon to give them a supply of water if they were ever besieged by Indians or pirates. Supposedly, church wealth was also hidden in this tunnel. Another variation related that when word was received to secularize the California missions, the San Diego fathers decided to transport their accumulated gold to Los Angeles. Two priests rode ahead of the mules loaded with the church gold. In one of the canyons just north of town, scouts spotted an Indian war party, and hurriedly unloaded the gold and concealed it in the cave. According to this version, the entire mission party was killed and the gold still rests in a cave, its entrance now hidden by a cave-in.

Though there is no proof to the story, it has long been believed that the Indians of San Gabriel Mission worked a secret gold mine in the San Gabriel Mountains north of Claremont. When it came time for the Mission San Gabriel Arcangel to secularize, the treasure was taken from the mission by Indians and carted to the hills where it was buried in what is now the town of Monterey Park.

There are many tales of treasure and lost mines associated with the missions around Santa Barbara and Ventura. One story told of an old Indian who used to regularly appear at the Mission Santa Ynez, located on the outskirts of Solvang, with large nuggets of gold to trade. Nothing could persuade him to tell where they came from, but he did say there were plenty more. Then there was the tale of the Franciscan padres taking fifteen mule loads of gold and silver with them when Santa Ynez mission closed. Supposedly, they buried the coins in rawhide bags at the bases of two giant oak trees near Aliso Ranch.

Like the mission fathers of San Gabriel, the padres in charge of the Mission Santa Barbara reportedly had Indians work a gold mine at the base of Ranger Peak, north of Lake Cachuma. Fearing the Indians would flee the mission with the gold, the priests told the natives there was a curse on the flaky ore. The exact location of this mine has not been found. However, there are records that Indians took gold from Piru Creek in the Santa Clara Valley near the San Buenaventura Mission in present day Ventura. Small quantities of gold are still found in this region.

Construction of the Mission San Juan Capistrano started in 1796 and finished in 1806. During its early days, the inhabitants of the village surrounding the mission declared war on Mexico because of the harsh treatment Mexican officials inflicted upon the Indians. Supposedly, a group of trusted Indians took church treasures into the hills and buried them. But when it came time to bring the treasures back to San Juan Capistrano, the Indians refused to do so, nor would they reveal where they had buried the mission valuables. In 1935, a search was made east of the town of Santa Ana. Although nothing was found, others claim the valuables were unearthed, but not reported.

The current mission at San Juan Capistrano was the second mission built in the area. The first, located in what is now the town of Mission Viejo, also has a treasure story. Reportedly, a treasure was buried when an Indian attack forced the missionaries to flee to San Diego for safety. As the tale goes, they buried their wealth under the foundations of an old building. When they returned to the mission, this treasure was left undisturbed for some reason. Later the old building was demolished, and when the second mission site was selected about five miles away, the treasure was forgotten.

The San Juan Capistrano mission also appears to have once had a gold mine which utilized Indian labor. It is believed that somewhere in the mountains east of the mission is a lost gold mine, the entrance sealed in an 1812 earthquake. Because several Indians lost their lives in this disaster, other members of their tribe refused to reopen the mine, which they viewed as their brothers' final resting place.

In 1859, a California pioneer named Daniel Sexton obtained permission to dig near the ruins of the San Juan Capistrano Mission for several bags of

Misión San Juan Capistrano
founded Nov. 1, 1776

Drawing of Henry Miller, Mission San Juan Capistrano, 1856 L.B.P.L.

gold he was sure were buried there. Giving no details as to how he knew about the gold, but assuring local authorities he would share his wealth, Sexton began to dig. And dig he did. He dug so extensively beneath one house that the owner began to feel the foundation give way, and Sexton was told he could dig no further. Sexton died insisting there was gold, and a lot of people guessed he knew what he was talking about, otherwise, he would not have done all that digging.

Few know that Southern California shores were terrorized by a French buccaneer, Hippolyte de Bouchard and his British partner Peter Corney in 1818. Since then rumors have circulated of stolen Spanish treasure buried here more than a century ago.

The Frenchman was commissioned as a privateer--a polite word for a pirate--by General Jose de San Martin, an Argentine revolutionary. In 1812, San Martin began his fight to expel the Spanish from all of South America. His successful campaigns allowed Argentina to declare its independence in 1816. The following year San Martin led an expedition across the Andes and surprised the Spanish troops in Chile. After the victory in Chile, his forces helped win independence for Peru. To finance this revolution San Martin needed Spanish treasure. One of the places ripe for plunder was sleepy Spanish California and its missions. The duo, and their crew of 300, hit Monterey and San Juan Capistrano, taking any valuables they could find. The people were frightened. Treasures were removed from remaining missions, women and children were evacuated and every attempt was made to capture the pirates.

There was panic in Santa Barbara when word was received that the pair were on their way to loot the village. Most people buried their valuables and headed inland to the Santa Ynez Mission where they felt they would be safe. One of those who tried to protect her jewels was Dona Josefa Boronda de Cota. She threw her possessions down the public well that once stood across Anacapa Street from the county courthouse. The well was then sixty feet deep, and after the pirates departed, no one would go down and recover the treasure. Money and jewels were reportedly still there when Dona Josefa died in 1882. Gradually the well filled in with debris, and a parking garage was ultimately built on the site.

With all of this looting, buccaneers Bouchard and Corney decided to safeguard their treasure in case of capture, and bury it along the California coast. According to legend, they arrived in the Long Beach area at night and came ashore to bury much of their gold, silver and jewels. No one knows for sure where they stashed their loot. However, there is reason to believe they chose Long Beach, because the area was unpopulated and off the main highway, El Camino Real (present day Anaheim Street). Perhaps they used Devil's Gate as a landmark. One side of the "gate" was a separate rock structure that extended seaward from the bluff, and the other was the bluff itself. Torn down in 1915 to build Belmont Pier, it was a prominent marker leading into the marshy area of

Alamitos Bay that would later be dredged to make Naples and Belmont Shore. However, no one knows where the riches were buried. The two died soon afterwards in South America, leaving the treasure behind somewhere in the Southern California area.

Devils Gate, 1905 H.S.L.B.

Deadman's Island

Deadman's Island, which disappeared when San Pedro Bay was dredged in the late 1920s, was a mystery island surrounded by legend and odd tales. The island was believed to be the burial place of Blackhawk, the last male survivor of San Nicholas Island. In 1846, after the Battle of Dominguez Field during the Mexican War, five men were killed by a band of rovers on the island and buried there. This murder was what gave the island its name.

The search for the pirate treasure became a popular hobby for anyone with time on their hands. In July 1906, it appeared as if a part of the fabled fortune was discovered. Two fisherman, Albert Fontuoa and Chester Howard, made a curious discovery on Deadman's Island--an eight inch square mahogany box.

Fontuoa and Howard, aware of the history and intrigue of the island, thought the box they uncovered might be a small part of the pirate loot, or some other treasure. They anxiously opened the chest only to drop it in horror. Inside was a man's skull, wrist and fingers. A rotted cloth that resembled red satin and looked as though it might have been an altar cloth at some time was also in the case. On one finger was a gold ring with the two letters "F.C." The island was living up to its name.

Some of the oldest inhabitants in the area were asked to shed light on the gruesome find. Local residents remembered a story about a feud in the 1850s between two Spanish landowners. For some reason, the Spaniards did not speak to one another. At a masquerade ball, the younger of the two, his identity shielded by his costume, had a friend introduce him to his enemy for a joke. The men shook hands. When the elder man found he had been tricked into talking to his enemy, he swore he would have the hand of the other man severed from his body while still alive, and he would bury it where it would never be found. Later the act was said to have been committed and the hand buried. The victim was Francisco Carlina (F.C.) and his remains were later interred in the Catholic cemetery at the old mission in Ventura County. It was suspected that the hand found by the fishermen was Carlina's, but where the skull came from could not be explained.

Portuguese Bend

In February 1913, a tourist by the name of P.C. Strong picked up a small copper spike at Portuguese Bend on the Palos Verdes Peninsula while he was on a whaling expedition with the infamous Captain J.D. Loop. Captain Loop and his seafaring buddies declared that no spikes of that type were used by modern ship builders. They were positive the relic dated back to one of the old Spanish ships which were made of oak timbers and fastened with copper. The spike was about eight inches long and badly bent. Was this interesting relic a piece of ship wreckage that had lain for an unknown amount of time in sand off the beach at Portuguese Bend? Could the ship possibly have contained valuable treasure or cargo?

The hunt for treasure continued. In 1952, C.W. Munson was convinced he had located pirate treasure at Portuguese Bend by using a dowser--a divining rod made of a forked green branch. For years rumors abounded that pirates once used the coves in the area for shelter, and that they left a metal box filled with Mexican gold, silver and jewels. The San Pedro man and four friends probed the hills for weeks searching for the right site, until Munson's dowser responded strongly in the Dead Man's Cove area. After digging 6 1/2 feet, the men found nothing more than dirt, rocks and their own sweat. Despite the bad luck, Munson was convinced there was treasure somewhere in the area.

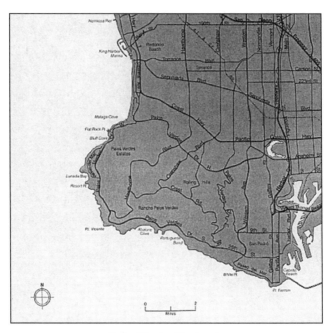

Palos Verdes Peninsula

Alamitos Bay Loot

In November 1924, when dredging was taking place in Alamitos Bay to remove silt deposited by the San Gabriel River, the blunt nose of a steam shovel made an interesting discovery--a skeleton buried in the channel flats in what is now Recreation Park. The men operating the steam shovel noticed a small wire enclosure, the size and shape of a grave, directly in the path of the dredger. Investigating the possible grave, the men found the remains of a heavy coffin and parts of a human skeleton. Transported to the Long Beach Health Department for identification, Dr. G.E. McDonald declared the bones were at least a hundred years old. Since dredging had destroyed the grave, McDonald ordered that the remains be cremated and scattered over the sea. Could the dead man have been a member of Bouchard and Corney's pirate ship? At least one of Bouchard's henchmen was reported to have laid aside his cutlass and forsaken his evil ways. Joseph Chapman, captured by the Spanish during one of the forays along the Santa Barbara coast, proved himself to be a model prisoner. He became a hard-working carpenter and millwright, and helped the mission fathers in their building. His diligence so impressed one woman, the lovely Guadalupe Ortega, that she later became his bride. But did Chapman also forsake the buried treasure? Did he ever return to claim the valuables stolen from the Spanish? Did he even know where Bouchard buried the plundered riches? We may never know.

We do know, however, that treasure in the form of gold was found in Alamitos Bay. In fact, the U.S. Land Office in Los Angeles was busily at work in October 1905 trying to determine whether or not there was enough gold in the ocean sand around Alamitos Bay and Anaheim Landing to class it with the other mineral districts of Southern California.

The Anaheim Landing Mining and Development Company was certain that a narrow strip of sand running out into the sea contained gold pure enough to fetch more than $100 per ton. The company sunk seven shafts, trying to prove there was enough gold in the black sand to make it mineral land, subject to state law and outside the reach of local landowners.

Though the Anaheim Landing Mining and Development Company could not convince the government to establish a separate mineral district for the Alamitos Bay area, they may have been right about the gold. On December 6, 1906, George Waterbury made a startling discovery when he turned the tap water on in his bath--liquid gold. Waterbury, knowledgeable about minerals, noticed his bathtub turned black when the water remained in it. As all users of the water from the Townsite of Alamitos (which was later to become part of Long Beach) knew, it was strongly impregnated with sulfur. This sulfur, Waterbury realized, acted as a good reduction agent when combined with other minerals. Waterbury filled three test tubes with the water and took them to a chemist in Los Angeles for analysis. The tests revealed the

Was Long Beach water rich in gold? L.B.P.L.

water contained gold. He was elated with his find and thought the water could be used profitably. However no one ever followed up on Waterbury's gold discovery, and the gold in the water remained unmined.

A treasure of a different sort, with no pirate connections, was discovered in the Alamitos Bay area of Naples in 1922. On August 3rd, following a severe grilling which lasted more than four hours, nineteen-year-old Waldemar Matmueller, the infamous Long Beach "Axe Burglar," confessed. Matmueller, who used an axe to smash his way into over forty homes, evaded police for over a year. With police persuasion, he drew a treasure map to guide the law enforcement officials to the booty. He revealed that a cigar box, full of jewels, was buried under a cement sidewalk. The rest was scattered over the fields adjacent to his Naples home. Police, armed with wire screens, rakes, shovels and other paraphernalia, dug for the stolen valuables. Diamonds, gold, pearls and platinum were recovered from various Naples lots. Law enforcement officers were never sure if they retrieved all of the loot. Some may still lay hidden in Naples to this day.

Catalina Island

Could there be buried treasure on Santa Catalina Island still waiting to be unearthed? We know there are at least three Manila galleons in the area. Could treasure from these wrecks have come ashore?

Early Avalon on Catalina Island, 1900's H.S.L.B.

Samuel Prentiss, a Rhode Islander, was one of the survivors of the brig *Danube*, which was wrecked off San Pedro in 1828. According to legend, an ailing Catalina Island Indian named Turai, at the San Gabriel Mission, befriended Prentiss and told him about a treasure trove on the island. The dying native drew a map for the shipwrecked sailor. He told Prentiss that tribal treasure and pirate loot from the missions were buried under a big tree. Prentiss anxiously sailed to Santa Catalina to dig for the "Pieces of Eight," but lost the map overboard. He soon tired of the hunt, built himself a cabin on a sunny hillside and lived there contentedly among the Indians for thirty years. He was the first white man buried on the island.

Was the treasure the Indian spoke of the same treasure Hippolyte de Bouchard and Peter Corney supposedly buried along the coast in 1818, or loot from the Manila galleons? No one knows. Before he died in 1854, Prentiss revealed to Santos Bouchette, the son of a sailor shipwrecked with Prentiss in San Pedro, the secret of the treasure. Bouchette was a man of action, and the fact that there is little timber on Santa Catalina may be due to the zealousness of his hunt. He is said to have cut around the roots of every big tree near Avalon and the isthmus because Prentiss told him there was a bay shown on the lost map.

Bouchette never found the buried treasure, which may still lie where a large tree once stood. However, he did find treasure of a sort when he uncovered a vein of silver. With samples of the ore, Bouchette went to the mainland and convinced others to invest in his mine. Andrew Jouglin, who amassed a small fortune in the newly opened port of San Pedro, supplied most of the money to purchase the equipment. Soon wealth poured in and Bouchette ended up marrying a French dancing girl. Although he built a large house for her on Catalina, the island life bored her, and around 1876 the Bouchettes sailed away and were never heard of again. In the fall of that year, Andrew Jouglin went to the island to look after his investment and found nothing but a deserted mining camp. He unearthed evidence that Bouchette had "watered" the vein, purposely deceiving investors and taking off with their money.

In the 1830s, while Samuel Prentiss was digging up trees looking for buried treasure, George Yount, a pioneer and sea otter hunter, chanced upon some gold-bearing rock on Catalina Island. Three times he went back to the island, the last being in 1854, looking for the lost lode. He could not find it again and his story brought a miners' stampede to Santa Catalina in 1863.

The Catalina gold rush quickly ended when the United States stepped in to prevent the island from becoming a gathering place for Confederate privateers. The Unionists transported gold from San Francisco around the Horn to the East Coast. Learning of this, the Confederates made plans to waylay the ships from a station on Catalina. The plan was discovered and a Union garrison was stationed on the island. The troops remained only about nine months, and soon the sheepherders and miners were back on the island. But the mining costs were too high and investors became wary as drought years brought depression to Southern California.

By 1887, the economy of the region improved. George Shatto bought the island and expected to make money by turning Timm's Landing into a resort. Because he did not think the name was very glamorous, he renamed it Avalon, the mystical land where King Arthur was said to dwell after his death. In the midst of Shatto's promotional schemes, an English syndicate, which believed there was still undiscovered gold on the island, offered Shatto $400,000. An installment of $100,000 was paid, but when an agent went to London to collect the balance the syndicate defaulted.

The days of treasure hunting and mining on Santa Catalina appeared to be over. In the late 1950s, however, interest picked up when diver Bob Retherford, who was testing watertight camera housings, came upon an interesting find. While checking the equipment off Catalina, Retherford chanced upon the anchor of what he thought was a sunken Spanish galleon. He told his tale to his friend Joe McCabe who excitedly joined Retherford in planning a thorough search.

In June 1960, what started off as a treasure hunt ended in tragedy when one of the members of the team drowned. As McCabe went down about 160 feet to tie a marker buoy to the wreckage, there was a foul-up in his apparatus and he drowned. Retherford and his skin diving wife, Shari, continued with the salvage operation. They believed the project was jinxed when they were caught by a sudden offshore storm that disabled their boat and tossed them seven miles off course for 5 1/2 hours. They were later rescued by a Coast Guard airplane.

The Retherfords could not forget Joe McCabe, who gave his life trying to solve the mystery of the sunken vessel. In 1961 they succeeded in retrieving the 12-foot, 3,000-pound anchor made of hand-wrought iron. Experts said it may have come from a Russian trawler, a Yankee clipper or even one of the Spanish galleons lost with countless millions in gold. The metal was the only clue, pointing to a forging date probably in the early 1700s. History buffs put the time of the wreck in the mid 1860s as this was a period of heavy shipping activity following the California gold rush.

What ship was it from? Only Retherford knew the exact location where he found the anchor. Did he discover more of the ship and possible treasure? Treasure hunters are frequently silent about their finds.

Treasure lies not far from Long Beach, on the floor of San Pedro Bay. On April 27, 1863, the steam tug *Ada Hancock* was transferring passengers from the wharf at San Pedro to the steamer *Senator*. Suddenly the tug careened, admitting cold water to the engine room. The boiler exploded, demolishing the vessel. Twenty-six of the fifty-three passengers aboard were lost, including William Ritchie, a Wells Fargo messenger who was carrying $10,000 in gold, and Fred E. Kerlin of Fort Tejon, California, who had $30,000. All available accounts indicated this money was never recovered and is still waiting discovery.

Point Argullo juts into the Pacific west of Lompoc. Because of prevalent fogs in the area, and the number of vessels that have met with disaster, it is known as the "Graveyard of the Pacific." On September 30, 1854, the 1,800 ton side wheel steamer *Yankee Blade* sailed from San Francisco with about 800 passengers and a steel vault holding gold bullion estimated in value at between $100,000 and $200,000. John Potter, author of *Treasure Diver's Guide*, wrote that no sooner had the ship reached the open ocean than she entered a dense fog. Twenty-four hours later, still advancing rapidly with her paddles going, the *Yankee Blade* struck a sharp rock which opened a seam in her bottom. She started to sink. Captain Harry Randell saw that the ship was doomed. During the night the sea rose. The stern broke and settled, and the foremast crashed down through the keel. The passengers, many drunk, spent the night on the half-sunken ship. The next day they were picked up by a passing steamer and delivered to San Diego. Two days later the *Yankee Blade* disappeared beneath the sea.

In *Treasure Guide to California*, Thomas Penfield added a twist to the story. Among the passengers bound for Panama, where they would be shuttled across the isthmus by wagon and board another steamer on the Atlantic side, was a band of criminals known as the Turner Mob. Their specialty consisted of boarding steamers as innocent passengers, seizing control of the ship at sea, and then beaching the vessel along a lonely stretch of coast where the cargo and passengers could be looted at will. Whether they, or a navigational error were the cause of the demise of the *Yankee Blade* is still debated. In any case, the money is supposedly still off Point Argullo sealed in a steel vault.

Gambling Ships

The Southland coast was an exciting place during the Prohibition years of the 1920s and 1930s. In 1919, the 18th Amendment to the Constitution outlawed the sale and transport of alcoholic beverages. Social reformers blamed alcohol for poverty and health problems. Employers felt that drunkenness reduced worker's safety and productivity. The 18th Amendment addressed these concerns; however, the Volstead Act, passed to enforce this amendment, was unsuccessful in stopping bootlegging and rum running. The illegal liquor trade was highly profitable and bootleggers battled each other for liquor supplies and markets. Furthermore, this contentious social and political climate fueled tensions among the underground crime organizations and violent gang wars erupted.

Johanna Smith, c. 1930 H.S.L.B.

Gambling ships stationed three miles off the coast were out of the jurisdiction of federal, state or local authorities. On these vessels, people could legally drink and gamble. The ships attracted a gangster element which horrified the "righteous" folk in the area. These law-abiding citizens hounded public officials to do something about this evil influence. In 1928, a Long Beach City Attorney uncovered an old Federal law buried since 1793, and decided to use it as ammunition against the floating casinos. Though originally aimed at piracy, it stated that any ship which failed to follow the activity provided in its license could be seized. The *Johanna Smith*, the first local gambling ship in the Long Beach area, was registered for coastwise trade however, she had been sitting in one spot for more than sixty days. How could she be engaging in commerce? It appeared she was in violation of her license

The *Johanna Smith* refused to move and was towed to the Long Beach harbor where she was held on a $200,000 bond. But the gambling contingent was smart. They outfitted a new gambling ship, the *Monfalcone*. The two vessels switched spots along the coast, giving the appearance they were engaging in coastwise trade, the stipulation of their license.

On August 30, 1930, 300 people barely escaped with their lives when the *Monfalcone* caught fire three miles off Belmont Shore. Fortunately, the *Johanna Smith* was anchored nearby. Rescue workers transferred the passengers to the other ship, preventing the loss of even a single life. But, the money on board the *Monfalcone* was not saved. About $40,000, mostly in silver coin, went down with the ship.

Salvage operations recovered only $3,000 in silver and bullion from the seventy-five-foot burial ground. Did the intense heat melt the remaining silver, making it hard for divers to discover? How much paper money was destroyed in the fire? Approximately $37,000 remains unaccounted for--still down there waiting for someone to find.

Gangsters and Gun Battles

The gambling ships and the men who ran them began to attract an "undesirable" element to the Southland. Organized crime stepped onto the scene, securing liquor for those not happy with Prohibition. Murder and the fear of being killed were tools used by these gangsters to control the trade in gambling, liquor, prostitution and drugs.

In 1929, duck hunters found an unidentified man whose heart had been blown out with explosives, in the Bolsa Chica area near Huntington Beach. At first, the police thought it was a ritual sacrifice of some weird religious cult. When they found another man buried alive a short distance away, they started to think it might have something to do with the criminal element lured to the area by the gambling ships.

Eventually, two men were arrested because they made the mistake of borrowing a shovel from a nearby dairyman to bury their victims. When questioned by police, they claimed it was not to dig graves, but to bury a box containing nitroglycerin, which they used in oil exploration. After further interrogation, the men revealed they used this nitroglycerin to blow safes. The body found without a heart had been a member of their gang. The fellow, not knowing how to handle the explosives properly, was blown away. The poor man that had been buried alive was also part of their gang. He refused to tell where money taken in a robbery was hidden. His two partners thought that putting him in a grave while still alive would frighten him enough to reveal the hiding place. They had planned to dig him up, but their timing was off. The loot, presumed to be somewhere in the ground, was never found. There may still be treasure somewhere around the Bolsa Chica area of Huntington Beach.

The gambling ship saga was to continue throughout the 1930s. In late December 1930, a Long Beach police officer, William Waggoner, was wounded and paralyzed from his waist on down by Chicago gangster Ralph Sheldon. Law enforcement officers thought if they could annoy the gamblers enough it would discourage them from going to the floating casinos. For instance, police forced the returning gamblers to undergo customs inspection and possible quarantine when coming back from the gaming vessels. As it so happened, Sheldon had kidnapped wealthy Hollywood gambler, Zeke Caress, and was on his way to the *Johanna Smith* to cash a check Caress had given him for his release. He did not know that the Long Beach police were doing their usual job of inconveniencing gambling ship patrons.

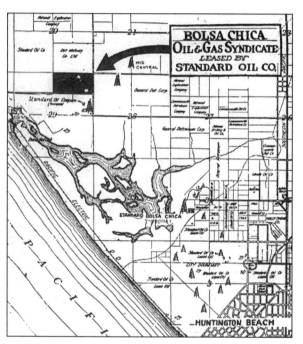

Bolsa Chica near Huntington Beach *L.B. Press* 4/1/1921

What ensued was a sensational gangland trial. It involved a record-breaking five week trial costing taxpayers $100,000. Why so much money? The prisoners were brought from Los Angeles and escorted by cars armed with machine guns. The exploits of Al Capone and the Chicago mob were still fresh in the minds of Southern California authorities. They did not want any drive-by killings or mob retaliations.

Sheldon and his pals were represented by expensive legal super stars determined to create a suspicion of "reasonable doubt" in the minds of the jury. In their first round, the attorneys were successful in getting the judge to tell the prosecution they could not bring up the fact that Sheldon had been arrested 124 times, but never convicted. Another point used in Sheldon's defense was that police officer Waggoner's partner carried the same kind of gun as Sheldon. Could it be possible that Waggoner's fellow officer had fired the gun that permanently paralyzed his colleague?

Eventually, enough "reasonable doubt" was planted in the minds of the jury, who also feared mob retaliation, that they acquitted Sheldon and his three accomplices. In the end, however, justice prevailed and Sheldon and his partners were convicted of the kidnapping of Zeke Caress and sentenced to ten years in jail.

The games between the gambling boat owners and local authorities continued. There were armed robberies and even murders aboard the vessels, but who had the legal authority to go after the bandits? The gambling ship owners were fighting in court to prove they were beyond federal and state law. If they were "beyond the law" why should local authorities go after the hold-up men?

Finally, in June 1939, California Attorney General Earl Warren announced he was launching a drive against the gambling ships operating off the Southern California coast. Though the United States Supreme Court refused to deal with the gambling ship problem, another recent Supreme Court decision gave Warren ammunition to make his move. He cited the U.S. Supreme Court decision *New Jersey vs. the City of New York*, which ruled that the dumping of garbage more than twenty miles from shore could be prohibited by the court of the State on whose shores the ocean current carried the garbage. Warren pointed out that the dumping of garbage in the Atlantic Ocean was not contrary to the law of any state or nation, and that the act of dumping garbage was prohibited solely on the ground that when it was washed ashore it became a *nuisance*. Taking the case one step further, Warren stated that because the maintenance of gambling created a *nuisance* in California, it was immaterial whether the gambling ships were within the three-mile limit or beyond. With this as his weapon, Warren launched his attack.

On August 1,1939, raids were led by police on gambling vessels off Belmont Shore. They met no resistance. The ship owners decided they would simply file appeals and take the fight back to the courts like they had always done. In Santa Monica things were different, thanks to Tony Cornero.

Tony Cornero, aboard his palatial gambling ship *Rex*, refused to let law enforcement officials shut him down during the August 1st raid. Cornero fought them off by shooting water from fire hoses. When this standoff was

Gambling ships would station themselves off Belmont Shore
Photo 5/23/1936 L.B.P.L.

reported to Earl Warren, he told his officers not to let anyone off the ship After all, there were women aboard whose husbands did not know they were out gambling, and there were men aboard whose wives did not know they were out with other women! After one night of the blockade, Cornero begged for mercy. Warren agreed to spare him the disagreeable death of being ripped apart by angry customers. A deal was made whereby his customers could come ashore anonymously, and Cornero could take his fight to court.

In the meantime, however, Warren had another idea. A world-wide economic crisis plunged the United States into a serious economic depression. The Great Depression, as it was called, was a worldwide business slump that began in October 1929 when stock values in the United States dropped rapidly. Thousands of stock holders lost large sums of money. The effects were far reaching forcing banks, factories and stores to close and millions to lose their jobs. During the economic troubles of the 1930s, many argued Prohibition took away jobs and deprived the government of badly needed revenues and taxes on liquor. On December 5, 1933, Prohibition ended with Congress passing the 21st Amendment. Throughout the 1930s, the County of Los Angeles issued innumerable relief checks for the care of poor families. Many of these checks ended up in the hands of the gambling ship owners. Now was the time for the County to try to get back some of this money. Los Angeles County was going to sue Cornero.

In December 1939, upon the advice of his counsel, Cornero gave up the fight. He agreed to the destruction of all the gambling paraphernalia aboard the *Rex*, to pay the State $13,200 for expenses incurred in putting him out of business, and to settle $4,200 worth of county taxes.

The reign of the gambling ships appeared to be over. With World War II beginning in Europe, ships were in short supply. The British, who lost many ships to the Germans, were willing to buy anything that would float. As a result, most of California's gambling vessels were converted to freighters hauling supplies for the war.

During the war years, Cornero served as a casino manager in Las Vegas. He was to reappear in 1946 in command of a new gambling ship, the *Lux*. Earl Warren, then governor of California, took up the fight again. He angrily wrote to President Truman complaining that Cornero was able to obtain the necessary steel, lumber and other materials that were in short supply due to the war. He asked Truman to help in ridding the California coastline of the public nuisance. Federal agents seized the *Lux* on a technical charge, and Cornero was relieved of his command. On April 28, 1948, Truman signed a bill prohibiting the operation of a gambling ship in the territorial waters of the United States. Cornero returned to Las Vegas where, in July 1955, he dropped dead of a heart attack after an all-night crap game in which he lost $10,000.

For twenty-eight years a forgotten treasure lay buried in the sandy bottom of Long Beach harbor. At one time it made international headlines and brought world attention to Long Beach. In 1944, a crew digging a new channel in the Craig Shipyard struck metal. To their astonishment, it turned out to be the remains of a 120-foot submarine developed here by inventor John M. Cage.

Old timers remembered the craft for breaking the world's submergence record in Long Beach harbor in 1913. It was the Germans, however, who saw the value of the design, adapted the submarine plans, and used American technology against the Allies during World War I. Allied submarine chasers, geared to listen only for the whine of electric motors, could not hear the murmur of the Cage gas engine. The German subs, using the Cage power system, could not be detected.

The story of this remarkable submarine dates back to 1911 when inventor John M. Cage began an active campaign to get area citizens to buy shares of his submarine stock. Models of his submarine were displayed with Long Beach merchants and ads placed in newspapers extolling the virtues of this modern invention. One hundred dollars in gold (housed at the First National Bank Building in Long Beach) was offered to any person who could discover any flaw, defect or imperfection in the theory and plans of the Cage Submarine Boat. His advertising campaign worked. Stock in the Los Angeles Submarine Boat Company, first offered at fifty cents a share, gradually rose to two dollars.

THE LAUNCHING

of the Cage Submarine Boat will take place at the ship yards and plant on the Inner Harbor (Parker avenue and Riverside drive,) Saturday morning at 5:30 o'clock, January 18, 1913, at high tide. The public is invited to attend.

The L. A. Submarine Boat Co.
Offices: 603-605-619-621 First National Bank Building. Entrance 621. Home Phone 84.

Announcing the launching
of the Cage Submarine
Long Beach Press 1/16/1913

By 1913, Cage raised enough money to build his dream machine and was ready to launch the prototype. The year was one of unusually high rainfall. By February 24th, more rain had fallen in a three-day period than ever before. A record 4.54 inches of rain turned the northwest section of Long Beach into one vast inland sea, and marooned residents had to be rescued.

Although the rain did not affect the launch of Long Beach's own submarine, a succession of "hard luck" accidents did. On January 18th, when Cage tried to launch his 75 foot, 42 ton, $44,000 steel submarine in the Long Beach harbor, 700 pounds of lead ballast, which had been insecurely placed, caused the boat to list to starboard. The hatchway opened and in came the water causing the vessel to sink. This was distressing to all those who backed Cage in his venture. On January 24th, the sunken boat was raised to the surface by means of barges and compressed air. Shareholders were anxious to see a successful launch and on March 7th, Cage ran an ad in the *Daily Telegram*:

> We have been rushing the repair work as fast as possible, and in a few days the boat will be demonstrating that the L.A. Submarine Boat Company's stock is really worth what we claim for it--$100 per share. All I ask is for an opportunity to show you, and then if you care to sell your stock I will buy it, and I will make you a better offer than you can get from any one else. See others, but before you sell, see me.[1]

Finally, on March 26, 1913, the submarine was successfully launched and submerged. Vitalized by his success and confident in his submarine, Cage was determined to break the world submergence record by twelve hours. The past record was held by the U.S. submarine *Octopus*, which on May 15, 1907, remained under water for twenty-four hours. Cage's plan was to stay on the bottom of the harbor for thirty-six hours (though he was sure the boat could stay down much longer if need be).

Cage submarine out of water *Scientific American* 8/25/1917

On June 10th, the eyes of the world were focused on Long Beach and the Cage submarine. About fifty people, including motion picture operators, officers of the submarine boat company, newspapermen and others gathered on the municipal dock at 5 a.m. to watch the Cage craft go down. Aboard her

Launching of the Cage Submarine (Cage is 3rd from right), 1913 L.B.P.L.

were John Milton Cage, attending to the submergence valve; his brother, Will D. Cage, operating the air and atmospheric valve; Captain Edward Dellringer, over-all supervisor; Engineer James Marshall; Guy V. Hoopengarner, manning the telegraph to the outside world; and Jack W. Wood, operating the valve leading to the compensating tank.

On-lookers were concerned about the quality and supply of air. Cage assured everyone that the craft contained much more oxygen than needed. There were twelve air flasks, with a capacity of 200 cubic feet, into which 20,000 cubic feet of air was placed. Inventor Cage estimated that each man would consume about twenty cubic feet of oxygen per hour. The engine room alone carried 720 cubic feet of air, enough to last the group of six men for six hours. Whenever the atmosphere became stale, the engines could be started and, in a few minutes, the entire boat would be reventilated. The old air would be forced out through the mechanical exhaust and the engine room filled with fresh oxygen. In addition, the submarine safely carried 41,000 cubic feet of air, over twice as much as was in the tanks.

On June 11th, 1913 at 5 p.m., using only ten pounds of air to lift the submarine from the thirty feet of miring mud at the bottom of Long Beach harbor, Cage was greeted by shouts and cheers from 10,000 people gathered to witness the finale of the record breaking submergence test. Long Beach mayor, I.S. Hatch, and J.P. Pitts stepped from the official launch to the top of the submarine and cut the seal placed on the hatch. A few seconds later the hatch was raised and the head of the young inventor came into view. All the men who had gone through the long test were in good shape except Mr. Hoopengarner, whose vigil at the telegraph key kept him up all night and caused his pained fingers to swell. Engineer Marshall showed the least ill effects from the trip, spending two hours on the Pike before going home.

Cage Submarine *Scientific American* 8/25/1917

Articles about this historic event in *Scientific American* and *Jane's Fighting Ships* promoted interest in Cage's submarine at home and abroad, but it brought no buyers. In December 1913, the submarine was impounded for unpaid debts and sold for $400, plus payment of $5,000 worth of bills, to the W.L. Cleveland Company of Los Angeles.

Patent rights to the Cage submarine were still held by the Los Angeles Submarine Boat Company. The company hired Abner R. Neff to act as its agent in selling their submarine design to the United States Navy. On January 5, 1915, Neff reported that the government gave the company the right to demonstrate the practical use of the submarine system. If the system, after thorough and exhaustive tests, proved satisfactory, Uncle Sam would pay a reasonable price for it. The bad news was that the builders had to assume all risks of failure.

Because of the company's past credit problems, the Secretary of the Navy asked for guarantees. Neff lined up other companies (which he refused to name) who promised to come up with the $150,000 to $200,000 to conduct the tests and take the financial risks for a share of projected profits. In return, the Los Angeles Submarine Boat Company turned the patents over to Neff in exchange for a share of future earnings. Neff, however, felt that a new system of propulsion was needed for the craft. From the original Cage design he developed the "Neff system."

The prototype Cage submarine, launched in 1913, came to a sad end. In January 1916, the craft sank in the Long Beach harbor. Three years earlier it made news worldwide, now it was to be scrapped for its steel plates. In February, Cage's former submarine was raised and dismantled. During World War I the hull was used as a storage tank for oil. In the course of time, the vessel was buried under several feet of earth and forgotten until 1944 when a crew of excavators began digging a new channel in the Craig Shipyard.

Cage, though forfeiting his rights to the submarine because of his financial problems, continued to invent. A new invention was the Cage six-cycle, three-phase silent engine:

> It has no valves, cam shafts or springs in the entire engine. There are no mechanical sounds when the engine is running and it is impossible to tell when the engine is running and it is impossible to tell when the engine is shooting ... Gas is taken through the engine with six positive working strokes and every cylinder produces a working stroke every revolution. The engine I have built weighs about 200 pounds and will develop 47 horsepower. It will make 30 or 35 miles per gallon of fuel in a car like the Ford or 24 miles in a heavier car. For marine work this engine will run in either direction. [2]

In 1915, John Cage moved his operations to Detroit to better his chances for marketing a patent for a six-cycle three phase automobile engine. But he was still tinkering with submarines. In November 1916, Cage was given an all-expenses paid trip to England to explain a new submarine design.

His latest submersible was somewhat different from the one he built in Long Beach. This one could stay continuously underwater for ninety days and maintain a uniform speed of thirty knots per hour submerged. Another feature of the submarine was that its periscope could be replaced in three seconds and for fifty-six successive times. The replacing of the periscope was one of the problems that bothered naval engineers for years.

Cage was hopeful he could convince the English that his submarine was the long expected ideal of an underwater craft. If successful, the inventor would receive a cash royalty of $100,000 for each vessel built. Unfortunately, the British did not buy. Abner Neff, with his adaptation of the original Cage design, was more fortunate. In May 1916, Neff convinced the United States Navy to purchase the submarine equipped with his "Neff" propulsion system.

Both the newly designed Cage system and Neff's did away with the use of storage batteries, which had been the cause of frequent submarine accidents. Instead, a gas engine was developed giving higher submerged speed and greater power of attack and escape. The lack of batteries meant freedom from the stinking, dead atmosphere of oil particles and acid smells. It was this novel gas engine system of which the United States government sought more research. In 1917, with the United States entering the war in Europe, the "Big Navy Bill" was passed. With it went an appropriation of $250,000, for building and installing an experimental set of machinery using the Neff plans in an already existing E-type submarine.

Operating mechanism of the Cage submarine
Scientific American 8/25/1917

In May 1917, Abner Neff returned to Southern California due to ill health. He asserted that German U-boats were already utilizing, with tremendous success, the principles of the submarine boat invented by John M. Cage and perfected by Neff himself.

The August 25, 1917 issue of *Scientific American* magazine published an illustrated write-up of the single power unit Cage submarine. The pictures showed the original Cage boat floating on an even keel and rising from the Long Beach harbor after its famous thirty-six-hour submergence. An interior view revealed the operating mechanism of the submarine and compared it to one the Germans were then using. *Scientific American* believed this photo presented definite proof the Germans were using the Cage propulsion system in their submarines.

Until his death in New Jersey in 1964, Cage continued his work. He was a prolific inventor holding more than 800 patents in electrical, chemical, biochemical and mechanical fields. The devices and techniques that he developed were eventually applied to submarine and space travel, television, national defense, lightning prevention, and cold remedies. He and his wife Lucretia Harvey had one child, the composer John Milton Cage Jr., who was widely known for his pioneering work in music.

Are there sunken World War II Japanese submarines lying somewhere off the Southern California coast? The government security surrounding them was so tight during the 1940s that it is hard to say.

Following the Japanese assault on Pearl Harbor on December 7, 1941, fear of imminent Japanese attack on the U.S. mainland was rampant.

Aerial shot of Long Beach harbor during WWII,
some areas blacked out L.B.P.L.

By December 24, 1941, enemy submarines in the Pacific off the California coast had attacked nine ships. On December 16, 1941, a tanker was torpedoed and sunk off the shores of Washington state. On succeeding days, other submarine attacks were reported in United States waters. Each strike was farther south than the preceding one. It appeared as if a single sub was cruising down the Pacific seeking targets. The assaults were always within twenty miles of shore and most of the time the enemy craft insolently surfaced for the attack.

North of Long Beach, off the coast of Cambria, the *Montebello* was heading north for Vancouver, British Columbia. Dick Quincy told *Preservation Magazine* reporters in their March 1997 issue, that the crew was told they might expect gunfire, as there had been an attack near Morro Bay. Just before 6 a.m. on December 23, 1941, Quincy spotted a "dark shape" emerging behind the tanker. It was too late to escape the approaching submarine, and within minutes a torpedo tore into the tanker's bow. All thirty-eight members of the *Montebello's* crew luckily survived. The tanker became one of three ships sunk off the west coast by Japanese submarines.

Long Beach Harbor 10/2/1945 L.B.P.L.

On Christmas Eve, 1941, a submarine appeared in the San Pedro Channel and fired a torpedo into the coastal steamer *Absaroka*. It was believed to have been the same submarine that attacked the *Montebello* on December 23rd. But was it the same submarine, or were there several enemy ships patrolling and attacking vessels along the United States mainland?

Soon after the sub was sighted it made an emergency dive. A bomb was dropped and the submarine emerged and then sank. Two more bombs were dropped, apparently scoring direct hits and filling the air and water with debris.

The *Absaroka* made port and was repaired. One of her seamen was killed when the torpedo explosion wrecked a portion of her deckload of lumber. The crewman was the only person killed by enemy action in coastal waters and was California's only casualty at home. (Later, members of an Oregon family were killed by the explosive charges attached to a Japanese stratosphere balloon they found in the forest).

A rumor surfaced on Christmas Eve, 1941 that an enemy sub was towed into Long Beach harbor. The report arose when a tug, hauling a barge of rock for use on the breakwater, was spotted at the same time the Navy was engaged in target practice. The rumor continued to grow. Within a few days people swore they had seen the enemy ship captured, towed into the harbor and worked on while in the boat yard. Could this have been the Japanese submarine that attacked the *Absaroka*? The Navy issued a statement warning about the spread of such wild rumors. Two weeks later posters appeared with the message, "Serve With Silence." This was to discourage "careless" talk about shipping and military operations in the harbor.

In April 1959, *Press-Telegram* reporter Bob Wells wrote of a conversation he had with William Kable, who served as a hard-hat deep-sea diver at the Long Beach Naval Station during the war. Kable related that he and another diver were sent to explore a Japanese submarine on the bottom, a few miles off the Cabrillo Beach end of the breakwater in 1942. The diver was familiar with the reports of the earlier raids on U.S. shipping along the coast and he presumed this was the sub that made the attacks. Kable was surprised, however, to find the enemy submarine to be a small one of the type usually used for coastal defense. It was manned only by six men. He was impressed with the valor of the crew who took the small boat so far and inflicted so much damage.

The bow was torn off, Kable said. He and the other diver entered through the conning tower. They took identification off the crew and removed the log and other papers. Kable believed the sub could be profitably raised for the quicksilver he reported was in the keel (the quicksilver provided a quickly shiftable type of ballast to make the craft faster). Kable went on to say that the submarine was resting on two huge rocks with torpedoes sticking out in the rear.

In May 1946, G.D. (Tonga) Stainbrook, a Long Beach diver, claimed he twice inspected the hulk of a submarine sunk in December 1941. It lay just outside a line between Point Fermin and Point Vicente under 180 feet of water. He claimed to have taken identification tags from the skeletons of several of the twenty Japanese in the shattered forepart of the vessel, turning them over to the

Red Cross so their government could be notified they were dead. Tonga Stainbrook said that he asked for, and received, permission from the federal government to salvage the submarine, but all attempts to raise the hull failed.

Could this have been the same submarine that William Kable found in 1942? Kable told reporter Bob Wells that the ship he discovered was a six-man submersible. Stainbrook's submarine carried a twenty-man crew. Both divers agreed, however, that the ships they found were damaged in the bow area. Was it the same vessel? Was there more than one submarine involved in the 1941 Christmas Eve attack?

In April 1942, an American Army bomber from General DeWitt's Western Defense Command attacked an enemy submarine in Santa Monica Bay. Residents of Hermosa Beach, Redondo Beach and Palos Verdes Estates watched twin-tailed P38 Lightnings of the 4th Interceptor Command sweep over the sea, dropping depth charges. Could this submarine also be off our coast, accounting for the discrepancy of the six-man vs. twenty-man submarine found around Point Fermin?

In 1955, salvage expert Steve Harrison considered raising the sunken vessel. Harrison was backed by businessmen from the Pike in Long Beach who were interested in exhibiting the craft. His plans were dealt a sharp blow, however, when the Navy told him the vessel was off limits to outside exploration. Reporter Bob Wells found the Navy's reaction to Harrison interesting inasmuch as the Navy had never officially admitted the submarine existed. When Congressman Craig Hosmer asked for information about the submarine, the Defense Department informed him that no enemy submarines were sunk farther south than the Aleutian Islands. And Japanese Admiralty records, the Navy said, gave no hint of a submarine operating off the continental Pacific Coast in December 1941. But why, in 1946, had Tonga Stainbrook been given permission to salvage the submarine and now, nine years later, Harrison was told by the Navy to keep away from whatever was down there?

We do know that real war did come to Southern California. It began at 2:24 a.m. on February 25, 1942. The shrill sound of air raid sirens broke the calm of Southern California and searchlights quickly split the sky. It was the climax of a frightening series of events. Ten Japanese submarines had reportedly been preying on merchant ships off the coast. At dusk on February 23rd, a submarine fired thirteen shells into the Goleta oil field near Santa Barbara. Navy Intelligence warned of an imminent attack on Los Angeles the next evening.

California was on the alert when radar detected an unidentified target 120 miles west of Los Angeles. Suddenly there was a flood of reports of enemy planes. At 3:06 a.m. a balloon carrying a red flare was reported over Santa Monica and four batteries of anti-aircraft guns fired at it. The air over Los Angeles erupted when between fifteen and thirty planes were reported near the Douglas Aircraft plant in Long Beach. At 3:20 a.m. anti-aircraft guns started shooting at these "unidentified objects." Fort MacArthur joined in, showering Terminal Island shipyards with debris.

Douglas Aircraft Plant in Long Beach during WWII H.S.L.B.

The firing continued for fifteen minutes and was resumed again at 4:06 a.m. for five minutes. Nearly 1,500 shells were reported fired. Not all of them exploded aloft. Two rounds detonated inside houses at 1741 Linden Avenue and 2036 Easy Avenue. Another damaged a Bank of America branch at 5401 Long Beach Boulevard. There were six indirect deaths. Three people died in traffic accidents, another three of heart attacks.

Was it a real enemy attack? Army Secretary Henry L. Stimson insisted there were up to fifteen enemy aircraft in the area. Navy Secretary Frank Knox said it was a false alarm. Some observers said they saw and heard the planes, others said they saw nothing. For years the "attack" remained a mystery;

however, years later Japanese records indicated that no submarine launched a war plane at Southern California that night.

Were there really Japanese submarines targeting the Southern California coast? On August 20, 1945, the war was over, but the Navy feared an attack by Japanese subs not happy with their country's surrender. A line of submarine nets was stretched across the outer entrance to the Los Angeles/Long Beach harbor. The Navy announced that objects that may have been Japanese submarines were detected in the harbor thirteen times. Depth bombs were dropped and oil slicks appeared, indicating that at least three of the prowling submarines were hit, but no wreckage or bodies came to the surface.

Twenty Japanese mines were found near the harbor entrance. All were believed to have floated across the Pacific. For precaution, a submarine net was draped from Long Beach's Rainbow Pier to the breakwater to cover both harbor mouths. Large buoys held in place by eight-ton anchors supported the 50,000 feet of net. The major gate at the harbor entrance could, however, be swung back and forth like a door to permit large vessels to enter, while the small craft unit off Rainbow Pier was raised and lowered like a curtain.

Though Japanese activity off the California coast was kept secret, one Long Beach man, Lt. Robert Clark Sweet was credited with sinking a Japanese submarine off San Clemente Island. Sweet was the commander of the Coast Guard cutter *Hermes* and patrolled thousands of miles of Pacific Ocean during the war. His job was antisubmarine surveillance, port protection and escort service. On August 12, 1945, the ship and her crew were awarded a bronze star for the sinking of an enemy submarine. The exact location and date of the successful submarine action was not disclosed by Coast Guard officials. They merely stated the victory was officially recognized by the Navy and that the bronze star rightly belonged to the *Hermes'* crew.

In September 1947, Navy divers descended fifty feet underwater near the east end of the Long Beach breakwater in search of a possible Japanese submarine. Herman M. Dillinder, a Long Beach photographer, spotted an object ten months earlier, but did not report it to the Coast Guard until September 25, 1947. Dillinder and a companion were en route to Newport Beach in a motorboat when they sighted what appeared to be the rusted remains of a periscope, conning tower and submarine bow. Dillinder said he did not report it because he assumed others would see it and alert the Navy of its presence. Months later, having heard nothing further, Dillinder reported the sighting, However, the object could no longer be found when he returned to the location.

After a four-day search in murky waters on the seaward side of the breakwater, Navy divers abandoned their search for the supposed Japanese submarine hulk. There was a supposition that the object viewed by Dillinder may have been one of the large number of surplus infantry landing craft disposed of offshore since they had conning towers similar to submarines. However, no vessel of any kind was found, only rocks.

In 1964, the Department of the Army published *The United States Army In World War II*, which looked at official Japanese documents for information about their activities during the war. In its prewar basic operations order of November 5, 1941, the Japanese Navy directed its 6th Fleet of submarines to make reconnaissance of the American Fleet in Hawaii and the West Coast area, and, by surprise attacks, disrupt shipping and lines of communication.

After the attack on Pearl Harbor, the 6th Fleet detached nine submarines to attack shipping along the California coast. Arriving there about December 17, 1941, official records reported the submarines were dispatched to nine stations from Cape Flattery in the north to San Diego in the south. If this is fact, the question about the December 16, 1941 attack in Washington state still remains unanswered. Claims were made at the time that an Army B-24 bomber also sank an enemy submarine on December 24th off the mouth of the Columbia River. Japanese documents reported that the submarine then assigned to this station was the one that returned eight months later to wind up enemy submarine operations off the Pacific coast. It, therefore, could not have been sunk.

According to the admiralty records, the fleet remained for about one week with only four of the nine submarines engaged in any known attacks on coastal shipping. The submarine detachment planned to engage in a simultaneous shelling of California coastal cities on December 24, 1941, but at the last moment Japanese Fleet headquarters ordered the force to abandon the plan and to withdraw immediately to its base at Kwajalein.

The Japanese reported that two of their submarines reached the west coast during February 1942. The first to arrive, the I-8, patrolled northward off San Francisco to the Washington coast. After encountering no enemy vessels, it returned to Japan. The second was the I-17, a plane-carrying submarine, which had already sunk one tanker in December. The I-17 arrived off San Diego around February 19th. On February 23rd, it surfaced off the California coast near Santa Barbara and fired at oil installations. Records from the night of the "Battle of Los Angeles," February 24-25, 1943, indicated that no Japanese submarine was there the evening of the attack.

California was warned of a more ambitious Japanese attack on the west coast following the Halsey-Doolittle raid on Tokyo in April of 1942. Fear of a counter attack was great. There was no mention in *The U.S. Army in World War II* of the Japanese having sent submarines here, so perhaps the sinking of the submarine off Redondo Beach during that time was incorrect. Maybe the incident was the result of overzealousness on the part of the military who thought it better to fire and be safe, than not fire and be sorry.

There was documented evidence that on the evening of June 21-22, 1942 a Japanese submarine fired shells at the Fort Stevens military reservation in Oregon, doing no damage. This shelling, insignificant in itself, was noted as the first foreign attack on a continental military installation since the War of 1812.

The final Japanese submarine operation off the west coast during the War, was undertaken expressly as a reprisal for the American bombardment of Tokyo in April 1942. The submarine I-25, carrying an airplane fitted for bombing, reached the Oregon coast late in August 1942. On September 9th, its plane dropped an incendiary bomb on a forested mountain slope near the coast at Brookings, Oregon. The bomb started a small forest fire, but this was quickly extinguished. Attempts to locate and destroy I-25 failed. After nearly a month of discreet hiding, the I-25 attacked and sank two tankers off the southern coast of Oregon on October 4th and 6th. These attacks marked an end to direct enemy activity off the west coast of the continental United States, although the Japanese were to plague the coast with their "free balloon" operations before the end of the War.

But what of possible sinkings of Japanese submarines? Published newspaper articles lead us to believe that Japanese subs were in our harbor. There was no mention in the Department of the Army publication about any sinking of Japanese submarines off the continental United States. But could the small subs supposedly found here be mini-subs from larger vessels? Japanese records said nothing about losses of midget submarines.

Contact with the Army's Center of Military History in Washington DC, indicated that a search of their files revealed limited information regarding the losses incurred by Japanese submarines off the coast of California. According to an unpublished Japanese account of its submarine operations, Military History Section, Headquarters, Army Forces Far East, Japanese Monograph No. 102, *Submarine Operations December 1941-April 1942*, (1952), the following Japanese submarines were active off the west coast: I-8, I-10, I-15, I-17, I-19, I-23, I-25, and I-26. Submarine I-10 was off San Diego; I-19 was off Los

Angeles; and I-17 was identified in the San Francisco area in February of 1942. Other submarines operated off the coast of Oregon and Washington. Of these submarines, according to the Japanese monograph, only I-23 was reported missing. It was reportedly sunk off Johnson Island by a U.S. submarine on April 26, 1942. All of the submarines were classified as either Fleet submarines, Large, or Fleet submarines, Small, with crews that varied from eighty to ninety-five men. Some of the larger submarines carried and could launch midget submarines.

Could some of these midget submarines be those sunk and discovered by divers in San Pedro Bay? In writing the U.S. Coast Guard regarding the medal awarded the crew of the *Hermes*, the following response was received from Scott T. Price:

> The answer to your question is very easy: *there were no Japanese submarines sunk off the coast of the United States.* Local newspapers were notorious for exaggerating wartime claims of sinkings. Also, many action reports filed by Navy and Coast Guard commanders claimed to have sunk submarines, both German in the Atlantic and Japanese in the Pacific, but post-war research has indicated that many of these "sinkings" in fact did not occur. The wreck you refer to is either misidentified or is the wreck of a U.S. submarine. Private scuba divers are the worst people to obtain information from. They exaggerate their findings to gain publicity, or in many cases, to obtain money from investors to aid in the salvage of otherwise historic shipwreck sites. Always take these claims with a giant grain of salt. [1]

Price did not answer my question about the medal awarded the *Hermes'* crew in 1945. Maybe that was also a fabrication.

San Pedro author and diver Torrance R. Parker, who wrote *20,000 Jobs Under the Sea: A History of Diving and Underwater Engineering,* agreed with the Coast Guard. When questioned about the submarines, he gave a similar response as the Coast Guard--there were not any. He also said that divers were notorious for stretching the truth. The U.S. Navy concurred with the Coast Guard and Parker, stating:

> During wartime, due to the `fog of war' it was, and still is common for belligerents to presume that enemy forces suffered greater losses than they actually did. We can not account for the claims of civilian divers, particularly with regard to identification of sunken vessels that may be badly damaged, corroded, encrusted with marine growth, partially buried, etc. [2]

The facts have been presented. The conclusions are up to the reader.

I f hunting for sunken World War II Japanese submarines, gambling ships or Spanish galleons, you may have a hard time. What you discover on your sonar may not be what you are looking for. For many years, the waters off our coast were used as a dumping ground for trash, old ships, ammunition and even atomic waste. Following World War II, many surplus ships were taken out into the San Pedro Channel and sunk. In 1960, 185 miles west-southwest of Long Beach, a vast undersea atomic dump was opened.

Today, using the ocean as a trash dump, especially for nuclear waste, is a controversial environmental issue. People living in the 1950s, however, took government safety precautions for granted. It was in this climate of public confidence with government safeguards that *Independent-Press-Telegram* reporter Herb Shannon wrote about the Seal Beach Naval Ammunition and Net Depot's disposal of explosives.

In 1955, Shannon told readers that enough abandoned explosive material to blow Long Beach off the face of the earth lay in a dumping ground only forty miles from the city. But these discarded bombs, shells, depth charges, and other explosives (with the combined power of an atom bomb) were not likely to cause trouble here or elsewhere. They were scattered over a hundred-square-mile area at the bottom of the ocean--midway between San Clemente Island and Santa Barbara Island, on the seaward side of Santa Catalina. In this area the ocean's average depth was about 600 fathoms, or more than half a mile straight down.

A ten-mile square area was selected as the Navy's official explosive dumping ground partly because of its depth and partly because it was out of normal shipping lanes. In constant use since it was established in 1944, an average of 100 tons of explosives a month were towed from the Seal Beach Naval Ammunition and Net Depot, and heaved overboard in the 1950s. A tremendous amount of overage and obsolete ammunition was dumped into the sea immediately after World War II. The Seal Beach Navy Depot continued to dispose of materials from all the Naval installations in the area, and from civilian ordinance contractors up to the 1970s.

Navy crews handling the disposal job received special hazard pay for this type of work. Selected for their familiarity with various types of explosives, they had to be qualified swimmers who did not get seasick. The materials were taken out on a barge-like craft called a "lighter," which was cut free from its tug and allowed to drift while the disposal work went on. When the last shell was dumped overboard, the tug returned to the lighter and towed it back to the harbor.

The ammunition depot was proud of its safety record. The depot pointed out they took pains to see that all the materials were processed for safety in handling, and packaged to make sure they would sink to the bottom. Some of the items, like flares and drift signals, came in cardboard containers and would float. The Navy repackaged all such materials in metal containers with holes in them to admit water. The Navy assured reporter Shannon that there was no possibility of any of the material coming back to shore. But some ammunition never left the shore.

In March 1958, the Navy told children playing around Sunset Beach to beware of live ammunition. Dredging in the area yielded live munitions that had accidentally fallen over the side of ships through the years when the explosives were being loaded and unloaded. To illustrate the dangers, the Navy staged a demonstration for about fifty children in a demolition area at the Seal Beach depot. The youngsters were shown the sizes and shapes of various ammunition casings so they would know what to look out for. Just in case this was not enough to deter youthful curiosity, several of the pieces were detonated to show the children what might happen if they decided to disobey "orders."

The depot, located along the southern edge of Seal Beach, became a prime Cold War target of the Soviet Union. In 1979, the U.S. government reported that a one megaton nuclear bomb exploding above Seal Beach would kill almost 500,000 people. The report fanned opposition to nuclear arms, and led many to pressure for the closure of the base. In a policy that continues today, the Navy refuses to confirm or deny the presence of nuclear ordinance. But a base official told *Orange County Register* reporter Gary Robbins that if a pleasure boat hit a munitions-filled barge in Anaheim Bay, the resulting explosion would probably wipe out neighboring Sunset Beach and create a new entrance to the bay.

Today, the 5,286-acre Seal Beach Naval Weapons Station provides two-thirds of the weapons carried by the Pacific fleet surface warships. Yet, the base is fighting the downsizing that has led to dozens of military base closures through the 1990s. On July 3, 1999, it became the last active-duty base in Orange County with the closure of the Marine Corps air stations in El Toro and Tustin.

PART 3

LONG BEACH
COASTAL LORE

The world began in Long Beach, in a sacred pool
on the Rancho Los Alamitos in the Indian village of Puvunga.
So many fish swam in the pool that the creators caused the water
to expand and become salty. Thus the ocean was formed.

Thomas B.Talbert *The historical volume and reference works covering*
Garden Grove, Santa Ana, Tustin, 1963.

I n the early days of its history, the seashore in Long Beach was something to behold--a solidly packed seven mile stretch of sand extending from the current harbor to Devil's Gate in what would later be known as Belmont Shore. Before there was a town, the shoreline was renowned as a fine picnicking ground. Families hitched a team of horses to a wagon and drove to the beach. While enjoying the salt air and salt water, they worked up an appetite for the picnic dinner by gathering clams, which they took home by the wagonload to divide among neighbors. Once in a while, visitors might spot a few cattle bones on the beach, remembering how during the terrible drought of the 1860s ranchers were forced to select a very few of the best of the herd to save and drove the rest over the bluff into the ocean.

Picnics on the beach in Long Beach, c1900 L.B.P.L.

116

Eventually a city developed, bringing to the seashore other enjoyments such as piers, and an amusement area known as the Pike. Visitors fished, participated in the debates of the Spit-and-Argue Club, bathed in the saltwater plunge, took a dip in the ocean, admired the sand sculptures of J.D. McCord, sat back and watched the sport of surfing, or enjoyed the carnival-like fun on the Pike.

Spit & Argue Club on Pine Ave. Pier, 1939 L.B.P.L.

Long Beach promoters pointed out that the city was a virtual Eden. It had a perfect climate. During the winter, Long Beach was warmer than interior towns because the Japanese current brought temperate waters from the Philippine Sea. As a result, January and February brought ideal beach weather. The city was cooler in summer than inland because of the presence of the sea. This was a great selling point in the days before air conditioning and central heating. All in all, Long Beach was a great place to spend some time.

Many people today do not know what Long Beach was like and wonder how things came to be the way they are. Few can even imagine a time before the breakwater, when Long Beach was a choice surfing spot and known as the Waikiki of the Southland. Fewer still know of the politics and intrigue that went into building one of the world's busiest ports. Let us step back in time and explore some tidbits of history. Let us find out about Long Beach's sacred stream, how the city almost became an island, the beginnings of the piers, harbor, Pike, Naples, and Belmont Shore. By understanding the past we can better understand the present.

In 1885, Long Beach's first pier was constructed at the foot of Magnolia Avenue on top of the clam beds picnickers so enjoyed. The $4,000 structure, built mainly as a fishing wharf, was reached by a flight of seven steps leading up from the sand. The pier proved such a success that it well repaid the cost. However, the weather and waves did deadly work on the wood and the pier gradually weakened. It was obvious it needed to be replaced.

Magnolia Avenue Pier, 1885 H.S.L.B.

The 1,200 citizens of Long Beach took action. They did not wait for a private business concern to erect a new pier in their village, but built one on their own with public funds. On July 11, 1892, the city held its first municipal bond election. By an overwhelming vote, the $15,000 bond to construct a new pier at the end of Pine Avenue passed. The fact that a mere hamlet passed such a large bond issue attracted nationwide attention. Long Beach entered the record books as being the first town in the nation to build a pier using municipal funds.

On Saturday, May 27, 1893, the Pine Avenue Pier formally opened to the public. It was an amusement pier with a merry-go-round, food vendors, and

118

novelty shops. There was something on the pier that appealed to tourists from all walks of life. Before long, other buildings sprang up around the pier, most notably the Pavilion (opening in 1899) for concerts and dancing. But worms ate the wooden pilings on the pier and annual repair costs averaged around $2,000. In 1904 the woodpiles were replaced with cement and a "new" Pine Avenue Pier was erected.

Long Beach Press 3/28/1921

The new pier was a great place to fish. There were days when the average fisherman pulled in 50 to 100 pounds of mackerel, herring or sole. At times, kingfish by the thousands were hauled from the sea. Waiting on the pier for handouts was Pelican Mike, one of the locals. The brown pelican first made his appearance around 1912 and through the mid 1920s was a regular feature at the pier. Postcards were made showing Mike at work begging for scraps of fish. Newspaper reports chronicled his arrival each year, and if he was late in returning to Long Beach, anxious citizens sent out scouts looking for him. J.R. Crape, owner of the Fisherman's Haunt, found Mike when the unusual bird was almost dead from hunger. A tear in his throat made swallowing food impossible and for days he was fed by hand, until the wound healed and he regained his strength. Crape's kindness pleased the bird, who made the pier his home (except for months when he flew away for some female company). Mike was polite in his requests for food. He waddled up to a fisherman, opened his mouth, and hoped the fellow got the idea that he was hungry. If ignored, Mike took hold of a trouser leg, hissed, and repeated his actions until he was fed.

Other Long Beach piers followed the one off Pine Avenue. In 1915, Devil's Gate, the rocky landmark before the Alamitos Peninsula, was destroyed to make way for the Belmont Pier. In the 1930s, residents decided to build a horseshoe shaped pier--Rainbow Pier--next to the Pine Avenue Pier (destroyed in 1934 by a storm). Rainbow Pier, too, met a sad end when it was torn down in 1966 to make way for redevelopment. Today only the Belmont Pier (remodeled in 1967, and scheduled for renovation beginning in the spring of 2000), built to lure Belmont Heights residents to join Long Beach, remains. However, memories of the past still linger. The small wharves built off Long Beach's Rainbow Harbor, next to the aquarium, were named for the famous piers of yesteryear.

Rainbow Pier & Auditorium, 1931 H.S.L.B

At the same time the "new" Pine Avenue Pier was being built, Charles Rivers Drake was creating an amusement area that would later be named the "Pike," after the "Ten Million Dollar Pike" at the 1904 St. Louis World's Fair. On the beach, from the Pine Avenue pier to Magnolia Street, Drake created a bustling, active, up-to-date Coney Island midway, with a playground and day nursery for children. West of the playground, Drake put in a monster Ferris Wheel, fifty feet high, the largest ever seen in this part of the country.

There were many transformations on the beach west of the pier in the spring of 1905. A boathouse was built at the water's edge immediately in front

Pike and beach, 1905 H.S.L.B.

of the bathhouse. A tower was placed on the boathouse where a lookout was stationed to let lifeboat crews know of any emergencies in the sea. In addition, a new rest pavilion was erected, with a sand floor and enough chairs and tables for 1,000 people. Here, visitors enjoyed their lunches in peace and comfort.

An aquarium was being constructed, similar to the one at Avalon. The two-story brick building was 30 x 126 feet, larger than the one on Catalina. It housed a vast number of glass tanks, containing nearly everything from a minnow to a whale, and specimens of every type of fish that could be found in local waters. A group of seals entertained visitors, but the aquarium was also a research facility. On the second floor was a fully equipped scientific library on marine life, which was open to all visitors.

A new skating rink, thirty-foot Ferris Wheel, roller coaster, and a penny arcade were ready for the 1905 summer season. The biggest hit, however, was an electrically lighted ride called "The Old Mill," a state of the art attraction in which boats in a water flume traveled through grottos and viewed various scenes.

The attire in the bathhouse reflected the latest trends. Sateen suits replaced all of the old style woolen bathing suits. The new chic models were red instead of the traditional black suits. When people complained about the revealing nature of the new suits, the Pike assured the public that everything at the Pike was clean, moral and entertaining.

Big breakers at Long Beach, 1905 H.S.L.B.

To celebrate the start of the summer season, the famous Professor Haddock demonstrated a new novelty--hot air ballooning. Professor Haddock who was equipped with a parachute, allowed the hot air balloon to climb about 500 feet before he jumped from the craft. Haddock fell a couple of hundred feet before his parachute opened and settled into a backyard. It was not an easy landing. Besides surprising the owner of the house, Haddock sprained his leg. But the show had to go on. Ignoring his pain, the aviator made another trip into the air the same afternoon.

The Professor should have called it quits after the first flight. During the second ascension things quickly went wrong as 100 feet off the ground the balloon started to deflate. Haddock realized he was in trouble and jumped. Barely forty feet above the ground his parachute opened, and Haddock landed safely a few feet from where he started.

Bathhouse on the Pike, 1905 L.B.P.L.

Before there was a Disneyland, the Pike was the place to go. Each year new attractions were added and enjoyed by generations of visitors and residents alike. If one did not have much money, that was fine. Anyone could wander around the Pike for free, enjoying the beach and the piers. Everyone returned home with fond memories of the good times they had.

The Pike was a tradition in Long Beach for seventy years. Unable to live up to competition from newer amusements, such as Disneyland, Sea World, Universal City and Knott's Berry Farm, it closed following the Labor Day weekend of 1979.

Today the Belmont Shore and Naples areas are two of the most vibrant and popular sections of Long Beach. It is hard to imagine that this bay area was once nothing more than a marsh, similar to the wetlands around Anaheim Bay and the Seal Beach Naval Weapons Station. In the 1880s, the only seaside landmass that stood above the water was the Alamitos Bay Peninsula.

In 1888, the Alamitos Land Company organized with the idea of building a harbor at the bay. Southern California was in the middle of a tremendous land boom. This, along with plans to bring in a railroad, fostered the belief that the Alamitos Land Company would lure the shipping business of Los Angeles valley to the natural harbor at Alamitos Bay.

The plan was to give the Los Angeles and Ocean Railroad, competitors to the Southern Pacific, a right of way through the land owned by the Alamitos Land Company around Signal Hill. Alamitos Bay was envisioned as the terminal point of the new railroad, and the bay a major harbor. By the end of January 1888, the Los Angeles and Ocean Railroad acquired the last link of land from Los Angeles. Rumors surfaced that six railroads, three of them transcontinental, planned to make Alamitos Bay their terminus.

On the heels of all these rumors, the Alamitos Land Company sold 200 lots around the peninsula. On February 5, 1888, the real estate frenzy began. Prospective buyers, purchasing a lot for $300, were told that it would be worth $1,000 to $3,000 in one year. In March, the first ship put into the bay and tested the depth of water. In April, plans were drawn up for a warehouse. By the end of July, however, things changed. At first, a "temporary" depression was reported, but in reality the Southern California real estate boom had collapsed. With it went plans for a port at Alamitos Bay. It was not until the development of Naples, nearly twenty years later, that interest in the bay picked up again.

Naples

Naples is perhaps one of the most unique districts in Long Beach, characterized by circuitous canals, expensive homes and an undefinable charm. It has not always been that way. Once upon a time it was nothing more than mud flats, and the only residents were fish, birds and other animals. The visionary who saw more than wetlands was Arthur M. Parsons.

The idea first formed while Parsons was hunting ducks on the salt marshlands of Alamitos Bay. Gazing at the watery terrain around him, Parsons thought about building a community in which canals wound in and out, similar to those in Naples, Italy. People thought Parsons was crazy. Tides passed over the area, covering what little land was visible at low tide. Yet, Parsons had a vision and he was determined to make it a reality.   It was not an easy undertaking. In 1905, there was no road into the area. All cement and gravel for the sidewalks and canals of Parson's new community were brought across Alamitos Bay on boats and barges. Most of the material for filling in the swampland came from Los Angeles. The lamp posts for Naples were hauled up Anaheim Road to the San Gabriel River bridge. At the bridge they were placed on boats and brought down the river at high tide. Avoiding the sandbars was difficult work.

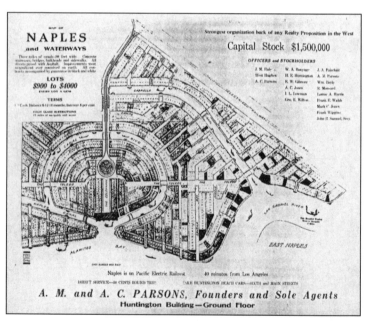

Original Naples real estate map, 1906 L.B.P.L.

The first house built in Naples, according to Walter Case in his newspaper column "Did You Know That--?, " was on the bayfront on the east side of Virg Walk. Built in 1906, the house belonged to Arthur C. Parsons, son of Naple founding father.

The canal builder himself, Arthur M. Parsons, worked on a house in 1905 at what would later be 4 Savona Walk. Though he poured $80,000 into its lacy fretwork and Moorish arches, he never finished it. Thirty-one years passed and an additional $125,000 was invested before Parsons' dream home was completed.

Naples, 1905 H.S.L.B.

Early residents of Naples quickly learned they had a long way to go for supplies. What the community needed were some stores, an electric car line and a hotel to house tourists. Henry Huntington entered the Naples picture in 1907 when his Huntington Land Company bought out Parsons. An economic depression struck California in 1906, brought on by the San Francisco earthquake. With Northern California's major city virtually destroyed, moneyed investors, who once put their funds into developing the south, moved their capital north to rebuild the ravaged metropolis. Parsons had a difficult time raising enough money to continue his dream and he was forced to sell out to transportation magnate Henry Huntington. It was a wise move for Naples' development, for Huntington brought with him his electric car line.

Naples Hotel, c.1910 H.S.L.B.

Miss Myra Hershey, of the Hershey chocolate family, opened a first-class hotel., and in 1907 Huntington's rail line extended directly to Hershey's Naple Hotel. This was wonderfully convenient for visitors. Myra Hershey quickly added a superior chef to her staff and the hotel's fish dinners became the talk of the town. People came from all around just to eat at the hotel's Pompean Cafe

Unfortunately, the economic recession brought on by the 1906 San Francisco earthquake was further reaching than first thought. The hotel close and the real estate activity around Naples came to a halt. Things remained stagnant until after World War I when Henry P. Barbour, working with realtor McGrath & Selover, placed the old bay resort of Naples on the map again

It was in this "new" Naples that one of the first "model" homes in Southern California opened in 1926. Called the "Press-Telegram Model Home," because of the financial sponsorship by the local newspaper, the ground breaking on September 3, 1925 was hailed as an important civic event. City official commended the *Press-Telegram*, and the thirty-three Long Beach firms who cooperatively built the house at 149 Siena Drive. The project inaugurated an educational campaign to interest the people of Long Beach in better homes. Th public, becoming more and more critical of the way houses were built, was demanding better architecture, better construction and more attention to modern conveniences. In addition, the mayor praised the developers for their foresight and vision in reclaiming valueless land and making it one of the most important residence sections of Long Beach.

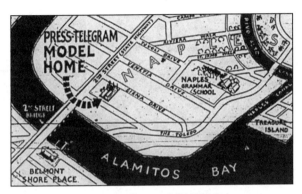

Press-Telegram 2/21/1926

For the next five months, the *Press-Telegram* kept readers informed of the construction details of this "model" home, opening the house for viewing on February 21, 1926. In March, the structure was put on the market for $18,000 unfurnished, $24,500 furnished. But the house did not sell. In November of 1927 the price was reduced to $12,500. On December 5, 1927, it was auctioned off for an unspecified amount. There was a new development just across the bay in an area becoming known as Belmont Shore. Here, for much less money, homeowners could apply the construction details they learned from the *Press-Telegram* articles on new homes of their own.

Belmont Shore

The Long Beach district now known as Belmont Shore was originally a soggy marsh surrounded by Belmont Heights and the Alamitos Bay Peninsula. Following World War I, and the discovery of oil on Signal Hill in 1921, optimism prevailed. Alamitos Bay was dredged and a new housing tract called Belmont Shore Place was created out of the former soggy soil by Samuel A. Delover and partner Warren McGrath.

Sales office for Belmont Park Tract - Second St. & Bay Shore Drive, 1923 H.S.L.B.

Realtors McGrath & Selover, who named their business the Belmont Pie
Tract company, began filling parts of Alamitos Bay in December 1919. The firs
lot (lot 4, block 23) in the initial ninety-nine acres of Belmont Shore Place wa
purchased by Miss Mary F. Mercredy in February 1920 for $2,750. In 120 day
the realtors sold most of the 1,060 lots and began work on phase two.

In July 15, 1922, the second phase, comprising 117 acres with 1,182 lots
opened. Salesmen stressed to would-be buyers that a 120-foot bridge of stee
and concrete, with a movable span in the center, would soon cross Alamito
channel. Also touted was the fact that the new state highway (Pacific Coas
Hwy) would be constructed down Second Street. To make the lots even mor
desirable, the Pacific Electric added a railway extension to the new community
These selling points worked and by 1924 the third phase, north of Second Stree
was put on the market.

By 1926, the entire area around Alamitos Bay was booming. Belmont Pie
Tract officials estimated that one new home was being built in their area ever

other day. Lots sold for $1,000 five years earlier were going for $3,000. It was time for McGrath & Selover to open another tract at the bay--Belmont Park.

Aerial view of Belmont Shore, including Belmont Pier, 1929 H.S.L.B.

On May 16, 1926, a ninety acre tract comprised of 530 lots, bound by The Toledo, Livingston, Bay Shore Avenue, and Appian Way were offered for sale. To doubly insure against the encroachment of oil development, a fear which halted residential development in other areas of Long Beach, restrictions forbidding oil drilling were placed in the deed to every lot in the tract. There were other stipulations. The lots on Broadway were designed to have approximately fifty-foot frontage and buyers had to agree to erect a two-story residence costing no less than $10,000. Outside of Broadway, building restrictions required homes be priced at $5,000 or more. To maintain the character of a residence park, the tract was zoned entirely for homes and apartments were not permitted. Duplexes, however, were allowed on the exterior tiers of the lots facing Livingston Drive.

Charles G. Adams, a landscape architect, was hired to lay out the planting scheme in Belmont Park. Part of the design called for every street to have its own type of tree. For example, Monterey Cypress was selected for Bay Shore Drive, while other tree varieties were used elsewhere so that all streets looked different.

Developer Samuel Selover built a home for himself in the new district. The unusual Selover Mansion, once located at 5420 E. Ocean Blvd., was the showplace of Belmont Shore. Its most unique feature was the basement, known nationally as "The Cave." "The Cave" was formed on three sides by a nineteen-foot-high sea wall that was also part of the mansion's foundation. The family patio served as the roof and an eighty-foot-long grotto with stalactites, crevices, pools and waterfalls formed the entranceway. Inside, the 20 by 33-foot room was specially illuminated with red, orange and blue lights that brightened or dimmed for varied effects. In the magnificent basement, the ceilings and walls were imbedded with quartz and ornamental rocks, while the floor was made of tile imported from Belgium. It also included a kitchenette, sewing room, music room, lounge, dressing rooms, shower, billiard table, fireplace and barbecue. Unfortunately, the unique residence was demolished in 1966 to provide additional beach facilities for the Belmont Shore area.

The Selover Mansion L.B.P.L.

The development of the Second Street business district began with a fruit stand on the north side of the street between Campo and Lauretta (in Naples) in 1923. It was quite successful, selling an average of 150 boxes of oranges daily. Area promoters believed this impressive sales record proved Second Street was destined to become one of the most important business arteries in Southern California.

In September 1926, it seemed that the prosperity of Second Street was assured when the Langford Block, the first two-story store and office building at the shore, was erected. Located on the southeast corner of Santa Fe, now Park Avenue, and Second Street, this Spanish-style building housed two large stores on the bottom floor, and two suites of offices and a large one-family apartment on the top floor.

Business growth took off in 1939, thanks to film stars Dick Powell and his wife Joan Blondell. The motion-picture pair purchased the entire 5000 block on the south side of Second Street between Granada and Argonne for a reported $64,500. The couple developed the lot as one architectural whole. In the center was a two-story building for the J.J. Newberry Company. The remaining buildings in the design were one-story. The Powell's investment was aptly named the "Miracle Block," because by 1940 the price of land along East Second Street increased 500 percent.

Businessmen and homeowners of Belmont Shore realized that architectural design and harmony was important to the community. In 1930,

Belmont Shore - Second Street and Livingston, 1930s H.S.L.B.

local residents banded together to defeat a proposal allowing apartments in the shore area. However, they could not fight Uncle Sam.

During World War II, Southern California experienced tremendous growth due to the defense industry. Between 1940 and 1944, the population of Long Beach increased 47.5 percent. Masses of people, still struggling to overcome the hard economic times of the Depression, flocked to Long Beach to work at the shipyards and aircraft plants. The population may have increased even more if there had been enough housing.

By 1942, war workers with families were turned away from Long Beach at the rate of 100 a day because there were no accommodations left for them. In spite of the fact that more and more workers came into the area as war industries expanded, the government halted all private housing construction, including housing built exclusively for war workers. The only government relief offered was barrack-type living accommodations, stripped to the barest essentials, and conversions of industrial and commercial buildings into temporary family units.

The War was the reason for the numerous duplexes and triplexes in Long Beach. Many Long Beach homeowners chopped up their residences into small units to help with war housing. Uncle Sam advanced the money to do so, interest free, and guaranteed owners tenancy for seven years. By June 1942, the United States government realized they had to allow some new residential construction. The problem of housing was so severe that many were unable to find a room or even a cot on which to sleep at night. Whole families found refuge in motion picture theaters, parks, libraries, or anywhere else they could rest. Most roamed the streets daily, fruitlessly searching for a roof over their heads.

The open land of Belmont Shore became one area on which government housing was built. Local residents were not happy when they heard news that permits for twenty-seven, four-family apartment houses were issued in their district. These apartments, built in the vacant block east of Livingston Drive and north of The Toledo, were the first units of fifty such buildings on three adjacent blocks. When completed, the project housed 200 families. Belmont Shore property owners were concerned that their real estate values would decrease because of these mass produced housing units (the design of which they also found ugly and repulsive). Nevertheless, the units were built and shore residents found they could not fight Uncle Sam--at least during times of war.

On September 8, 1542, sixty-seven years before Henry Hudson discovered New York Bay, Cabrillo sailed into the Bay of San Pedro and anchored his two ships, the *San Salvador* and *La Vittoria*. Up until the gold rush days, San Pedro Bay was the most important commercial port in California., and few vessels visited the coast without calling at it. Besides being the embarcadero of three important missions--San Fernando, San Gabriel and San Juan Capistrano--it was the port of the largest town in California--Los Angeles.

By 1887, the inlet at San Pedro had several rivals. In that year, Collis P. Huntington and his Southern Pacific railroad concern purchased several hundred acres of land along Santa Monica Bay. At Redondo Beach, Huntington and his partners built a substantial pier and a rail line to the city of Los Angeles. Other harbors were also developing at Newport Beach, Anaheim Landing, and Alamitos Bay.

What was really needed to handle the increased shipping for the growing Los Angeles area was a deep port--not simply a pier to dock at or a shallow harbor in which to anchor. Such a port would necessitate vast outlays of money that only the federal government could provide. The question was--where to put the harbor?

There were many players in the Los Angeles harbor fight. On one side the Southern Pacific Railroad, under Collis P. Huntington, stood as the most powerful proponent of locating the harbor in Santa Monica, where Huntington had heavy investments. On the other side stood those in support of San Pedro, many of them involved in businesses with motives hardly less mercenary or self-serving than those of the Southern Pacific. Included in the pro San Pedro contingent was the Los Angeles Terminal Railway Company and business interests from Long Beach.

Both sides battled it out for the better part of a decade. In 1892, the Secretary of War appointed a board of five engineers to look into the matter. They unanimously selected San Pedro Bay. However, Huntington protested the choice and secured a second committee, which, unsurprisingly, decided on Santa Monica. This angered the citizens of Los Angeles to such an extent that they formed The Free Harbor League of Los Angeles, which petitioned Congress to select San Pedro Bay. Their efforts secured the deep harbor port for San Pedro Bay. It was viewed by many as the people's victory over the Southern Pacific "octopus."

Rock being deposited on breakwater, 1942 L.B.P.L.

To celebrate this victory, a festival called "San Pedro Day" was held on April 26, 1899. At 11 a.m. the harbor jubilee began when President McKinley, at the White House, pressed an electric button signaling the deposit of the first rock on the breakwater site. The historic event did not go as planned. When guns were fired announcing President McKinley pressed the key, water gates opened on the barge to free the rocks. Unfortunately, the rocks did not break loose. An anxious crowd of 20,000 cheered, whistled and waved when the rocks, pushed in by the crew of the *Hercules*, finally began rolling, tumbling and splashing into the water.

The entertainment lasted all day, culminating with a firework display at 8 p.m. The *Los Angeles Times* reported that across the bay the lights of Long Beach "glittered like a long string of jewels," and that the citizens of the city, to show they were not at all envious of the prosperity which was now San Pedro's, kept up a display of fireworks on the waterfront.

Schemes & Plots

Long Beach's joint efforts with Los Angeles, San Pedro and Wilmington successfully brought the harbor to their bay, and away from Santa Monica. But Long Beach and Los Angeles were both jealous of San Pedro, as their actions in future years would show. Long Beach entered a battle with San Pedro for control of Terminal Island. Los Angeles, eager for a harbor of its own, cunningly annexed San Pedro on August 13, 1909 and Wilmington in September of the same year.

Harbor and the Los Angeles River, 1938 L.B.P.L.

Los Angeles began its "march to the sea" in 1906, when it gobbled up a half-mile strip of territory touching San Pedro that used to belong to the town of Gardena. There was much speculation as to what area Los Angeles would develop first, San Pedro representing the outer harbor and Wilmington the inner harbor.

Henry E. Huntington and his Uncle Collis, who fought a hard battle to have the government funded harbor built in Santa Monica instead of San Pedro, finally conceded defeat. In August 1905, H.E. Huntington took out a fifty-year lease on outer harbor property in San Pedro. In exchange, Huntington promised to build terminals, wharves and warehouses. He also pledged to bring his commercial business enterprises from Santa Monica to San Pedro. He envisioned his Pacific Electric railway carrying all local freight, and his Southern Pacific railroads handling the transcontinental cargo.

The consolidation of San Pedro and Wilmington with Los Angeles was, predictably, a highly sensitive proposal. Many in the smaller two cities were aghast at the idea of losing their identity and being absorbed by the big city to the north. However, the package they were offered was overwhelmingly attractive. Los Angeles vowed to spend $10,000,000 in harbor improvements over the next ten years. They also promised both towns a modern fire station, fully equipped police station, a public library, and an up-to-date school system. In case there were any second thoughts, Los Angeles officials reminded the citizens of San Pedro and Wilmington that Los Angeles recently annexed Harbor City. This gave Los Angeles actual frontage on the bay and a place to start its own harbor should San Pedro and Wilmington refuse to see the light. Perhaps this added "leverage" was what helped settle the matter, for both towns approved the annexation.

For years, the two communities strove to retain their separate identities. In 1921, San Pedro residents, businessmen and officials were fighting mad when they found out that Los Angeles was trying to abolish the names of San Pedro and Wilmington, and have the whole harbor district, except Long Beach harbor, known as Los Angeles Harbor. Their protests were for naught however, as the entire San Pedro Bay became known as the Los Angeles/Long Beach Harbor area.

Long Beach, too, was involved in schemes to establish itself as a harbor presence. In 1902, the Pacific Electric rail line came to Long Beach and the town experienced tremendous growth--by 1910 the census revealed it to be the fastest growing city in the United States. The Red Car allowed people to get to Los Angeles (or to Long Beach) in just twenty minutes. One could live at the beach and work in the city. Realizing Long Beach's potential, two real estate promoters, Dana Burks and Henry Barbour, cast their eyes on the Long Beach side of San Pedro Bay. When Burks and Barbour obtained an option from Stephen Townsend and C.J. Walker on their new Riverside real estate tract in the west part of Long Beach in 1905, it was with the idea of developing a resort, not a commercial harbor. Aware of the work then under way at Venice, where lagoons and canals were being laid out for entertainment purposes, they thought that a similar project could be done at Long Beach.

At about the same time, Arthur M. Parsons was developing a canal system at Alamitos Bay, and Naples was launched. Burks and Barbour thought that the competition was too close and decided to concentrate on building a commercial harbor in what was then called Cerritos Slough. Dredging of the slough and various channels and slips was proposed. One suggestion was that the north and south canal, dug to create a Long Beach inner harbor, continue around Signal Hill to Alamitos Bay. Long Beach, in effect, would have been made an island. The projected costs however, proved too costly and the idea was abandoned.

Secret Land Dealings

Instead of a canal around Signal Hill, Barbour and Burks sought commercial opportunities for the harbor. Both were well aware that the United States had taken over the rights to dig a canal through Panama in 1904. Once the Panama Canal was finished, untold wealth awaited ports on the western seaboard. At the time, the tide flats of Long Beach were connected with the navigable channels of San Pedro's Inner Harbor by Cerritos Slough, a tidal channel 60 to 100 feet in width, and navigable for shallow craft at mean tide. The Los Angeles River and its outlet to the ocean were blocked by the trestle bridge of the Salt Lake Railroad and the estuary by a dam. Access to the ocean was, therefore, limited to the tortuous channel of Cerritos Slough by way of Wilmington and San Pedro.

Burks' and Barbour's initial plan envisioned a horseshoe canal, using the river as far as Sixth or Seventh Street, and turning back to the bay so that ships could steam in one way and go out the other, without the necessity of building a turning basin. They later revised their plan and proposed a main channel, with a depth of 32 feet at mean low tide, and 400 feet wide. Two lateral channels, 21 feet deep and 300 feet wide, were designed for the dockage of coastwise vessels and smaller sized trans-oceanic ships, while the main channel was reserved for larger trans-oceanic craft. A turning basin was to be constructed north of the entrance.

To accomplish their goal of creating a commercial harbor, Burks and Barbour, and their newly formed Los Angeles Dock & Terminal Company, devised a scheme in which they secretly bought the marshlands surrounding their envisioned harbor. Wetland owners, who had little use for these partially submerged lands, sold at a good price. The company's secret plan was to fill in this land with silt from the dredged area and create the inner harbor's waterfront, wharfage and industrial zone. Once completed, Long Beach would have more dockage area than neighboring San Pedro.

138

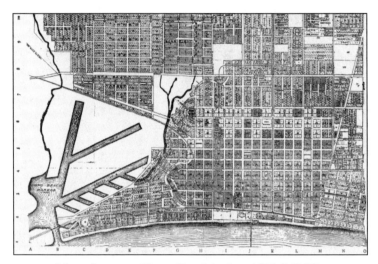

Map of proposed Long Beach harbor, 1906 L.B.P.L.

In the summer of 1906, hints circulated that a syndicate was thinking of purchasing the Watson-Dominguez ranch, which was comprised of 600 acres of land between Wilmington and the San Gabriel River, north of Anaheim Road. In August, the rumor was put to rest. Word was released that the acreage was sold, and that the purchasers were none other than the Los Angeles Dock & Terminal Company.

The purchased property was some distance away from the waterfront, but it did not take more than a look at a map to see the possibilities of future harbor expansion into the newly acquired territory. The closing of this deal meant that there was no more acreage left in the harbor district. Slowly, the promoters' plans were unfolding. Not only would Long Beach have a harbor, but a great manufacturing district as well.

Dredging of the harbor began on December 12, 1905, but it was not until January 6, 1906 that an official celebration was held. Over 2,000 people, along with members of the Los Angeles Dock & Terminal Company, attended this "Harbor Celebration." All in attendance agreed that Long Beach harbor was destined to be the greatest on the Pacific Coast. The Reverend Charles Pease summed up the feelings of those in attendance:

> I am sure we may all congratulate ourselves that which is inaugurated at the present time will be for us beyond that which we have ever dared to dream ... and that this day may be more significant than any Long Beach has ever yet passed in her history.

and go down to posterity as the day which marked the inauguration of a period when the great pumping engine down on the flats began to throw mud and pile it up and increase the acres so valuable to us, and which only a few years hence will demonstrate are all too few. *1*

Less than a week later, the Los Angeles Dock & Terminal Company moved their offices from Los Angeles to Long Beach to be closer to the harbor operations. At the same time they paid off, in cash, all of the owners of the wetlands on which they were to build the port. It was reassuring to the people of Long Beach that the company was financially secure. However, questions as to their fiscal responsibility would arise with the troubles of Henry Barbour.

Weeks after the harbor celebration, news came that struck like a bolt of lightning--Henry P. Barbour had been removed from his position as a member of the Board of Directors of the Los Angeles Dock & Terminal Company. The real estate developer's financial matters became so tangled that creditors attached much of his tangible holdings. He was also threatened with criminal prosecution as a result of some of his business dealings. When the Dock & Terminal Company got wind of the complaints, they confronted Barbour and demanded his resignation. Barbour's refusal caused the board to vote him out of office.

Dana Burks blamed Henry Barbour's big heart for his troubles. Barbour, known as a liberal spender, often promised more than he could deliver. Many of his financial problems came with his promise to beautify the bluff area of Long Beach in exchange for title to build there. The area remained an eyesore because Barbour ran out of money. Barbour was involved in numerous real estate ventures, and his financial situation became so tangled he was unable to pay many of the original landowners of housing tracts he developed. It was these people who were going after him with criminal charges.

Rumors spread that Barbour fled the country. When it was discovered he was in Mexico, Barbour claimed he was there for a vacation, and was planning to pay off all his debts. True to his word, Barbour returned to the United States and, in October 1906, was brought to trial. Murray Mitchell, Barbour's private secretary, who knew all of his secrets, was now the one who was missing. Mitchell fled the area pursued by police. Fortunately, before he vanished, Mitchell gave authorities a sworn statement, spicing the story up by disclosing Barbour's "blonde lady friend" and their "vacation" together in Mexico.

Mitchell claimed he collected $10,000 worth of stock in the Dock & Terminal Company while Barbour was in Mexico, money that rightfully belonged to Barbour's creditors. According to Mitchell, Barbour intended to divide most of the money between his lawful wife and his "friend" May Nye. Mitchell believed this was being done to conceal the money from Barbour's creditors. Whenever any of the stock was sold, Mitchell said he was told to send the money to a Fred Bristow, Barbour's financial advisor and a mining promoter. However, Mitchell disappeared, and Bristow, if he ever existed, did as well. There was no money, and Barbour was forced to declare bankruptcy.

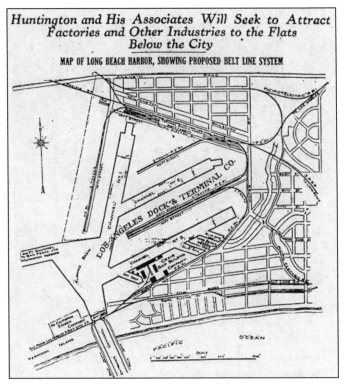

Map of harbor *Daily Telegram* 7/15/1910

Dana Burks assured everyone that Barbour was in no way, allowed access to Dock & Terminal Company funds. In fact, most agreed the company strengthened its position by getting rid of Barbour. However, Burks' earlier statement about Barbour having a big heart would prove to be true--Barbour did pay off all of his debts even after declaring bankruptcy. Henry Barbour would go on to become a pillar of Long Beach society.

Human Barricade

Dredging of the Long Beach harbor started in December 1905, but not all were happy with what the Los Angeles Dock & Terminal Company was doing, especially those who felt they had been duped by the company into selling their marsh lands at a cheap price.

On August 13, 1906, a woman and a sixteen-year-old boy placed themselves directly in front of the dredger and refused to move. At issue was a fight over the ownership of the salt marsh, which was being dredged. The original owners of the San Pedro Salt Works claimed the land belonged to them as they had leased it from the Seaside Water Company, and that they had not been paid for the rights to dig it up. The representatives from the Dock & Terminal Company said that they had already secured the land from the Salt Works. But who owned the Salt Works? The founders of the San Pedro Salt Works secured a lease on the disputed territory and agreed to pay the Seaside Water company a rental amount and taxes semi-annually. If they did not, the lease would be forfeited. No money was received for a period of two years. In the meantime, both the Salt Works and the territory passed into new hands. The Land and Navigation Company held it for one and a half years, selling it with clear title to the Los Angeles Dock & Terminal Company.

The first owners of the Salt Works suddenly decided to offer the Seaside Water Company the back rent on the lease. The Seaside Water Company, upset at the manipulative way the Dock & Terminal Company and the Land and Navigation Company persuaded them to sell the land, agreed to accept the back rent. They then claimed that the land was not legally theirs to sell. Though neither Seaside, nor the original owners of Salt Lake had a lawful leg to stand on, they hoped to delay the construction of the harbor by tying the matter up in the courts.

The Long Beach harbor contingent, however, managed to get a court order to continue dredging. That was when the Dunn family entered the picture. Mr. Dunn, angry at the little money he received for his wetlands, appeared on the dike and leveled his Winchester rifle at the man on the dredger. Work stopped. Later, officers came and arrested Dunn, but his daughter-in-law continued the protest. She placed herself in the direct path of the dredger's scoop so that it could not operate without hurting her. Another Dunn relative placed himself on the dike to deter the dredger from digging in that direction. The captain of the dredger ordered that the Dunns not be touched, or hurt, and the woman lying in front of them be treated with all courtesy (they admired her spunk). The dredger then turned and began working near the bank where the boy sat. The earth around the lad began to crumble and he quickly left. The dredging machine then began to pile up dirt and mud in a bank near the woman's position. Before the woman was forced to flee, an attorney for the Dunns appeared and took her away.

A quick legal decision cleared the matter up. The land clearly belonged to the Los Angeles Dock & Terminal Company. Nothing was going to stop their plans--not even a human barricade.

First Large Tenant - Craig Shipbuilding

In 1906, John F. Craig, a second-generation shipbuilder from Toledo, Ohio, visited Long Beach. The growth and development of the area impressed him and he was well aware of the tremendous opportunity the opening of the Panama Canal would bring to a western port. Craig decided to relocate his shipbuilding company to the California seaboard, if the price was right. Lured by $300,000 in relocation costs and forty acres of free harbor land, Craig chose Long Beach over San Diego. On February 27, 1907, the contract was signed. Craig was just what the Los Angeles Dock & Terminal Company needed--a large tenant for the new industrial tract of the harbor. But it was a united effort that brought the experienced shipbuilder to Long Beach.

On January 16, 1907, a mass meeting held at the municipal auditorium resulted in raising over $100,000 to lure Craig westward to Long Beach. Everyone contributed, including two Chinese proprietors of a laundry, who gave

Craig Shipyard, 1910 L.B.P.L

$25 from their meager earnings to the cause. This, coupled with later monies pledged by other citizens and businesses in Long Beach, completed the citizen's part of the deal. All the Dock & Terminal Company had to do was complete their landfill of the harbor industrial zone. By 1909, the inner harbor, comprised of four miles of still water between a depth of 20 to 30 feet at low tide, was complete. The ocean entrance at the mouth of the San Gabriel River was opened, allowing access for large sea vessels. Craig could start his shipyard.

The first buildings Craig erected were a machine shop, foundry, office and powerhouse. In the machine shop all the equipment used to construct ships was made. At first, the company hired 100 men, but within two years they were employing from 400 to 500 shipbuilders. Most were local men and their salaries were spent in Long Beach, boosting the local economy. Securing the shipyard was a real coup for the city--it was the only steel shipyard south of San Francisco. Long Beach was beginning to draw wide attention to itself as a maritime presence.

John F. Craig, whose father was also a shipbuilder, was born in Gibraltar, Michigan May 18, 1868. He made his home in Long Beach for more than forty years before passing away on January 5, 1952, at the age of eighty-three. Craig did much for the city in that time. In 1910, he organized the Los Angeles Dredging Company and the Western Dredging and Marine Construction Company, which kept the harbor navigable and free of silt. During World War I, when the government was desperate for ships, Craig swung his organization into action, turning out fifteen cargo vessels and three submarines. He came to the country's rescue once again in World War II, gearing his shipyard up to full production, turning out ships at a tremendous rate. When the Harbor Commission was created in 1931, Craig was named chairman, a post he held until his failing health forced him to retire. Long Beach did well in luring this man to its shores.

Harbor Dedication

On Saturday, June 24, 1911, the Port of Long Beach opened for business. With the steamship *Santa Barbara* lying along side, and a portion of her lumber cargo unloaded upon the wharf, the $240,000 municipal docks were formally dedicated. Though this was not the first cargo to arrive and be unloaded on the city piers, the fact that the vessel was one of the largest that ever entered the harbor was a cause for celebration.

A good-sized crowd gathered to listen to the music of the Municipal Band and the various speeches describing this momentous event. Captain Zaddart of the *Santa Barbara* was invited on an automobile ride about the city and entertained by numerous city officials at a luncheon at the Virginia Hotel. With the arrival of the *Santa Barbara*, Long Beach showed the outside world that there was a harbor of note on the Pacific ready for business and able to handle it when it came.

First ship to dock in Long Beach harbor, 1911 L.B.P.L.

Most of the credit went to the Long Beach Improvement Company, organized on March 11, 1911. When the government turned down requests for federal funds to develop the harbor (on the basis that it was nothing more than a real estate promotion), local men stepped onto the scene. Composed of many Long Beach business men, including Mayor Windham, bankers P.E. Hatch, C.J. Walker, B.F. Tucker, D.M. Cate, J.P. Curtis, R.H. Young and realty dealers, Stephen Townsend, J.H. Betts and T.G. Harriman, a company was created to construct houses. It was lumber for these residences that the *Santa Barbara* was delivering. Earlier, the Long Beach Improvement Company sounded the harbor and proved that big ships could safely come in. They also established lumberyards and a mill on the harbor to prepare for a much anticipated construction boom.

On October 17, 1911, President Taft, whom city fathers unsuccessfully tried to lure to Long Beach in 1909, honored the city with a visit. His speech was brief, but he made a specific promise of governmental aid for the Long Beach harbor.

Bridging the Harbor

The growth of the harbor necessitated the need for a new bridge, one that would clear the passage to the outer harbor. In 1909, the Salt Lake railroad opened their $250,000 bascule drawbridge. The single span was 180 feet long, making it one of the largest single-span drawbridges constructed up to that time.

The Salt Lake railroad (which would eventually become the Union Pacific) made a wise move. Much of the land that the railroad secured in 1891, when they first came to the harbor area, proved extremely profitable. The railroad sold property to the Ford Motor Company, Spencer Kellogg and Sons and the Southern California Edison Company. Most fortuitous was the discovery of oil on its Terminal Island properties later in the century.

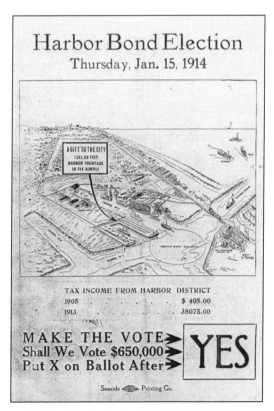

Harbor bond election 1/15/1914 L.B.P.L.

One of the problems confronting harbor development was drainage from inland flooding. From 1893 to 1904, Southern California passed through a period of drought, and the San Gabriel River was dry. Even during the wet years, from 1904 to 1910, no flood water reached either the river or the harbor. But things changed. The meandering Los Angeles River, causing frequent floods during wet years, needed a permanent course. Its outlet to the sea would be Long Beach. In 1911, the Los Angeles River flooded, sending silt-laden water into Channel No. 3. In 1914, the same river caused a disastrous flood which reduced the navigable channels to sloughs. Eventually, in 1920, the Los Angeles River Flood Control Channel was built, offering permanent protection from floodwaters for the harbor.

The Los Angeles Dock & Terminal Company continued to develop the harbor, selling its major holdings to D.M. Reynolds and Associates in 1923. In 1937, the company changed its name to the original, substituting Long Beach in the title instead of Los Angeles. It cost a lot of money to keep the three inner channels, the turning basin, and the entrance channel in navigable condition. It was only the continued sale of property that enabled the firm to defray the costs.

Aerial photo showing harbor bascule bridge & Edison Plant, 1920 L.B.P.L.

Following the 1906 San Francisco earthquake, the booming economy of Southern California took a tumble. All of the investment money headed northward to rebuild the city by the bay. The Los Angeles Dock & Terminal Company ran into financial difficulties and required help from the City of Long Beach. Long Beach realized it needed to take a role in harbor development. On September 9, 1909, the first Long Beach municipal bond for harbor and commercial development passed by a six-to-one margin. The amount of $245,000 was issued--$200,000 for purchasing 2,200 feet of frontage on Channel 3 and the rest for construction of a wharf on the same location.

There were sacrifices in harbor development. By March 1911, an island known by a variety of names from "Consolidated" to "Goosetown Lighthouse," but generally known as just "The Island," disappeared. It was in the channel for more years than people could remember. During flood runoffs from the San Gabriel River the island washed away. Now it was just a memory.

Panama Canal Opens

On October 10, 1913, at exactly five minutes before 11 a.m., factory whistles blew, auto horns tooted, flags unfurled, and Long Beach engaged in wild pandemonium--the Panama Canal opened. All morning the Chamber of Commerce kept in touch with newspaper offices. They wanted to make sure the correct time President Wilson touched the button in Washington, signaling the destruction of the Gamboa dike in Panama. The destruction of the Gamboa dike technically meant that the Panama Canal was completed, but it was not until August 15, 1914 that the 10,000-ton steamship *Ancon* became the first big ocean-going vessel to travel through the canal.

At daybreak on August 16, 1914, the *Lasata* cruised out of Gatun Lake and through the canal. Though newspapers reported the *Arizonan* and *Missourian* of the American-Hawaiian steamship line were the first private vessels through the canal, they were wrong. The *Lasata* was the first, and she had the toll receipt to prove it.

On September 6, 1914, the ninety-foot cruiser *Lasata* arrived home in Long Beach after a 6,000-mile cruise. Morgan Adams, owner of the *Lasata*, proudly showed a $57 toll receipt from the administrative office of the Panama Canal. Written across the receipt was: "For the first ship through the Panama Canal." Only the *Ancona*, the official government boat, preceded it, by merely a few hours. Friends and relatives gathered at the Long Beach wharf inspecting the scrap of paper that looked like a check. All agreed that it was one of the most desirable trophies a Californian could want, a historic treasure to cherish.

Long Beach was proud of Morgan Adams' accomplishment and with Long Beach's port. With cooperation and drive, it achieved in little more than a decade what took San Pedro twice as long to accomplish. San Pedro Bay was now home to two ports. Competition brewed. Which side of the bay would be the center of harbor activity? Was there enough commerce for both to survive? Time would tell. But maybe Long Beach, with her "sacred stream," the Cerritos Slough, would have a spiritual advantage.

Long Beach's Sacred Waters

In March 1911, people wondered if the waters of the Cerritos Slough, which fed into the harbor, were sacred. A religious sect from Fendlay, Ohio seemed to think so. The Reverend John W. Hurley, of the Revived Spiritualists, claimed a spirit voice, speaking through a trumpet, commanded the group to seek the promised land. They were to bathe in the healing waters of the sacred stream, located two miles from the city of Los Angeles.

Long Beach's sacred waters - Cerritos Slough, 1915 H.S.L.B.

The group believed the spirit voice was the Reverend Freed, who "passed over" several years earlier and communicated with the believers at their nightly sittings. All twenty-six members decided to follow his orders. One woman sold a $6,000 farm in Michigan for about half of what it was worth in order to raise the money to come to California. The group said they wanted no publicity, and had they not been questioned by newspapermen who learned that a special rail car was chartered for the trip west, they would have kept their quest quiet.

The Revived Spiritualists believed their ultimate destination was Jerusalem. However, the group asserted they would not be told to journey there until after they obeyed the first of the heaven-sent decrees--to bathe in the waters of Southern California's sacred stream. The Revived Spiritualists arrived in Long Beach and bathed in the supposedly sacred waters of Cerritos Slough, but whether they received other heaven-sent decrees, which eventually led them to Jerusalem, remained unknown. But others, too, came to believe in the healing qualities of Long Beach water.

In 1916, Wray E. Meyer of Tucson, Arizona wrote to the Long Beach Chamber of Commerce, asking that a five-gallon jug of Long Beach water be shipped to him each week by express delivery. Cost was no object. It was Meyer's belief that Long Beach water helped cure his wife's chronic stomach and bowel trouble. While vacationing in Long Beach, the family enjoyed the soft sulfuric water that local residents got to taste every day. Meyer and his family were planning to move to Long Beach, the "fountain of health," as soon as he could get his business dealings settled.

Cerritos Slough eventually disappeared when the harbor expanded, dispersing the "sacred" waters.

Separating the San Pedro and Long Beach harbors was Terminal Island. Formerly known as Rattlesnake Island, the island continued to be the battling ground not only between poisonous reptiles and residents, but between the cities of Long Beach and San Pedro (which would be annexed by the City of Los Angeles in 1909).

Business expanded in the City of Long Beach with the advent of the harbor. Long Beach was out to form a greater community labeled by the press "Greater Long Beach." City officials wanted to move the western boundary to the eastern shore of San Pedro Bay. To do so meant annexing Terminal Island, which was attempted in 1905. San Pedro officials were incensed at the annexation attempt. The fight was hot at the Terminal Island polling place, Johnny Wray, State Senator W.H. Savage and other San Pedro politicians entered the fray and tried to swing the vote of the territory against annexation to Long Beach. They wanted to set up their own annexation plan so that San Pedro could control Terminal Island.

When it came time to count the 146 ballots, five of them were found to be "irregular." The "no" cross on one was in lead pencil, instead of stamped in ink, and four other ballots were stamped a little off the line provided (three of these had voted "yes," and one "no.") Throwing out these five ballots, the vote stood 71 against annexation and 70 for annexation. An anxious period followed. If the election board said the ballots should stand as marked, it was clear that the election would result in a tie. Each side argued their claims. The board finally threw out the pencil marked ballot and decided to count the others according to the apparent intent of the votes, adding three to the annexationists' vote and one to that of the anti-annexationists. The vote was 73 for, 72 against.

Most recognized the importance of this election because with the acquisition of Terminal Island, Long Beach truly became a harbor city. The city would stand to gain control of all the water frontage on the east side of the bay from the inner bay to Deadman's Island. It looked like Terminal Island was now part of Long Beach, but the San Pedro contingent claimed they would fight the annexation all the way to the Supreme Court. In the meantime, they went ahead with their own election to acquire Terminal Island. The war was on. Long Beach claimed San Pedro had no right to hold an election to annex land that legally belonged to Long Beach, and San Pedro lived up to their promise to take Long Beach to court. Eventually, through numerous legal battles, the island was divided between the two cities on opposite ends of the bay, Long Beach claimed half, while San Pedro, then part of Los Angeles, claimed the other.

What was Terminal Island like in the early days of the twentieth century? At low tide one could wade across the river outlet to Terminal Island from Long Beach. However, all of this would change with the enlargement of the entrance channel to the new harbor.

JANUARY 25, 1926   THE LONG BEACH MORNING SUN

Terminal Island and harbor, 1926 *LB Sun* 1/25/1926

Terminal Island was an interesting place. The beachfront was set aside for housing. A block or so behind the houses lay the Salt Lake railroad tracks and beyond that some desolate looking land, which had a hard time raising weeds. Back a little farther were a number of boathouses, a canning factory, an abalone processing plant and further to the west, two big lumber companies and their mills.

It was the abalone business that was most important to the island. Eight or nine divers went out in their suits daily, harvesting the univalve shellfish. At the height of the season, from twelve to fifteen tons of abalone were handled weekly. Some were boiled for canning, others dried by steam. W.W. Beach, the owner of the abalone processing plant, developed a unique way of steaming. Terminal Island was the only place where the abalone was dried this way, and the result was very pleasing to the palate. The shells were also used, ground up for poultry food or fertilizer. The perfect shells were turned over to the California Pearl Manufacturing Company and transformed into ornaments. Many were made into brooches, belt buckles and earrings and sent to curio and jewelry stores throughout the United States.

The Terminal Island of 1906 could not be called a city, and it would be hardly fair to call it a village. Although the population was small, it had a good school that went up to the eighth grade with about eighty-five pupils and two teachers. When not in school, the local youth enjoyed a novel pastime-- rattlesnake hunting. A battle between the snakes and the inhabitants of Terminal Island occurred in April 1908 when the venomous creatures took possession of homes, yards, streets and fields. The residents were terror stricken. Over the years they became somewhat used to rattlesnakes, but the reptiles propagated so rapidly that the human inhabitants did not know how to deal with them. Long Beach officials estimated there were over 800 snakes on the island, despite all the city's efforts to get rid of them. Hearing this, local schoolboys decided to give the exterminators a hand. Once school let out, youngsters organized themselves into fighting squads and, armed with clubs, went snake hunting. On a good day, the boys killed as many as fifty snakes in a single afternoon. Fortunately, the youngsters knew their snakes and no fatalities occurred from bites.

There was not a lot of entertainment for children, except for the large bathhouse, pavilion and pier extending into the ocean. The island did not have many stores operating only a butcher shop and general store. At one time there was a bar, but the citizens voted in 1907 to outlaw alcohol on their island. It was a nice place to live, but fairly dull since liquor was banned from the island and most of the rattlesnakes killed. Things would change for Terminal Island, however, when the fishing industry decided to make it the center of their operations.

In October 1904, Loring B. Haskell, a Gloucester, Massachusett fisherman, decided to make the move to the Pacific coast. Haskell had already developed a large fishing business in the east and was quite excited about the potential he saw in California. Haskell thought the harbor area would be perfect for establishing an extensive fishing industry.

In 1937 there were 235 industries in Long Beach, including this cannery on Terminal Island H.S.L.B.

Before this time fishing was done on a small scale, principally by Italians living in San Pedro. There were about fifty small fishing boats, each carrying from two to three men. A cannery, the California Fish Company, started in 1892 on Terminal Island helped process the catch. Haskell decided to follow the example employed on the Atlantic coast where bigger vessels were utilized with greater carrying capacity and larger crews. These craft operated on fishing grounds that were further out, and followed schools of fish in their migratory movements. These larger vessels not only furnished the public a steady and sufficient supply of fresh fish, but also lowered prices and expanded the market. One of these larger ships could bring in more fish than all the San Pedro fleet of 1904 combined. Haskell's revolutionary ideas transformed fishing on the West

Coast, but there was still room for small boat owners to make a decent living as the American public discovered a love for tuna.

The tuna industry began in 1906 when Terminal Island's California Fish Company decided to expand its canning operations and take advantage of the large numbers of fish Haskell's methods were bringing into the plant. Company owners A.P. Halfhill and R.D. Wade tried canning yellowtail, rock cod, barracuda, halibut and a few other varieties of fish before discovering the pleasing qualities of tuna. The fish was not only nourishing, but it tasted good and packed well. The public loved it and soon canned tuna was a staple food in the nation's market. In 1912 three new canneries opened in the harbor area to meet the demand for "chicken of the sea". Tuna fishing became an attractive and profitable occupation. Orange growers, bank clerks, carpenters, and men in various other occupations tried to get into the "tuna game." They were lured by stories, founded on fact, of fabulous returns for their investments. Crews of the smallest boats ran up a take of $3,300 to $7,500 in the five-month season from June 1st to November 1st. Quite a lot of money for the time. By 1915, the Los Angeles-Long Beach harbor area, with twelve canneries, was the center of the industry.

Canneries were important on Terminal Island   L.B.P.L.

In 1915, a new method of catching tuna was instituted--seining. A fishing net, with floaters at the upper edge and sinkers at the lower, was hung vertically in the water. The fish entered and the net was drawn shut. Before seining, a hook and line was used, but it was limited because of the use of live bait. The seine method was more effective, capturing many more fish.

The canneries surrounding San Pedro Bay were state-of-the art. The Van Camp SeaFood Company, at San Pedro, for example, was equipped with big conveyors, which unloaded five tons of fish from a boat in five minutes. Once in the cannery, the fish were placed into cookers, which boiled out the oil and loosened the bones. Then the meat was lifted out in big hunks and packed in salad oil and salt.

The fish cannery industry looked to Terminal Island as a good location for processing plants. In 1915, rock was brought in from Catalina Island quarries to fill in the western edge of the Terminal Island wetlands. When they were finished a small harbor, called Fish Harbor, was formed. The Russell-Greene-Foell Company completed the first dock at Fish Harbor that same year. The wharf cost $360,000 and dredging work an additional $171,342. Railroad tracks were run into the area in 1916 and sewers and lighting installed in 1918. By the start of World War II, Terminal Island was the largest fish-canning center in the world.

Japanese-American Fishing Village - Tami-na-ru

Twelve men from Wakayama, Japan arrived in the San Pedro area in 1900 and started a Japanese community that would eventually thrive on Terminal Island.† By 1907, other Japanese fishermen joined these original abalone divers to work in the expanding fish trade Loring Haskell created. These first generation immigrants known as Issei came from Wakayama, Shizuoka, Taiji, Katsuura, Wabuka, Tanabe, Shimozato, and Shingu, Japan. Bound by language and customs, 150 Japanese settled close to the canneries on Terminal Island in 1915, creating the community known as Fish Harbor (Tami-na-ru, in Japanese).

† C. Robert Ryono in his book *Although Patriotic, We Were Drydocked*, says 12-15 men from Wakayama, Japan started the abalone industry at White Point in San Pedro in 1900, though the exact number is debated by the Japanese Community.

At the outbreak of World War II, Fish Harbor on Terminal Island was mainly a Japanese settlement, boasting more than 1,500 fishing vessels. They ranged from small one-man dories to big 120-ton tuna clippers carrying crews of fifteen or more. By 1940, boundaries of the tiny little harbor, built especially for the fishing industry, were lined with docks, crowded with boats and backed up to huge packing plants, an oil station, boat-building shops, supply houses, stores and cafes. Japanese, Filipinos, Italians, Slovenians, Russians, Mexicans and many more nationalities were found there. However, it was 2,600 Japanese that formed the backbone of the fishing colony.

Fishermen's Hall was the center of civic activity on Terminal Island, a place where Islanders could go for Judo tournaments, festivals, and movies. Two hardware stores, Hashimoto and Hama, had a common door toward the front of their shared building so a person could wander from one store to the other. Community spirit prompted residents to buy equally from each merchant. Half hidden by shrubs and trees on one street of Fish Harbor was a Daigingu Temple, a quaint Japanese style building surrounded by beautiful gardens containing white plaster statuary. Dwarf Japanese trees and shrubs adorned the front of a store which bore Japanese lettering. Visitors could see a Japanese newspaper office, a school and people dressed in asian attire. The local school included kindergarten thorough seventh grade. C. Robert Ryono, who attended school in Fish Harbor during the 1930s, remembered the student body was 99.9 percent Japanese with only two Caucasian students. The teachers, however, spoke no Japanese and the parents could not speak English. Despite this language barrier, Ryono recalled that the relationship between the teachers and parents was warm, and a close kinship developed. Indeed, the closeness of the Japanese community with the educators was the envy of other school communities.

This idyllic life came to an end on December 7, 1941. Japanese pilots bombed Pearl Harbor, catapulting the United States into World War II. Campaigns for patriotism included distributing anti-Japanese pamphlets and posters. All of this fostered negative attitudes and stereotypes regarding the growing Japanese population within the United States. Situated between Reeves Field (the Naval Air Base), and the Federal Correctional Institute (where Al Capone was once a prisoner), Fish Harbor was of strategic importance following the United States' entry into the war. Some in Washington saw the Japanese village as a nerve center for foreign espionage. Following the attack on Pearl Harbor, the area was closely guarded by government troops. Japanese fishermen were not allowed to go out in their boats to fish for fear they would contact the enemy. However they were allowed to continue their work in the canneries. On December 9, 1941, Frank Ishii, president of the Long Beach chapter of the Japanese-American Citizens League, spoke for the League's 1,000 Japanese members in pledging support of the United States in its war with Japan. Despite Ishii's assurances, most Americans viewed any Asian as a possible spy or saboteur.

Fish Harbor underwent what was perhaps one of the government's most extreme wartime policies. On February 4, 1942 the Federal Bureau of investigation (FBI) staged a raid on Fish Harbor to round up those who had not registered with the federal government as aliens. Because of language barriers, many Terminal Island fishermen were not aware of the procedures involved in registration. As a result, 339 men were incarcerated at the federal prison on Terminal Island. On February 21, 1942, FBI agents and local police throughout the Pacific states arrested hundreds of registered enemy aliens, including alleged pro-Nazis, Fascists and Japanese militarists. Twenty-eight alien Japanese were rounded up in Long Beach by the FBI. In only one instance did they find contraband - a short wave radio set covered with dirt, dust and rust. The set did not look like it had been used in a long time. Also, on February 21st the government issued a condemnation order on Fish Harbor to make way for expansion of the Navy base. This was the end of the Japanese colony on Terminal Island.

Many Japanese and Japanese-Americans refer to February 19, 1942 as "the day of betrayal," to signify the date when President Franklin Delano Roosevelt signed Executive Order 9066, establishing a 200 mile coastal military zone and barring people of Japanese descent from the region. On March 30, 1942, the Western Defense Command, following this Executive Order, instructed all Japanese, American-born and alien, to be out of the Long Beach area before noon April 5. Ten "relocation" centers were established at Manzanar, Tule Lake, and Granada, in California; at Poston and Gila River, in Arizona; at Minidoka, Idaho; at Topaz, Utah; at Hart Mountain, Wyoming; and at Jerome and Rohmer, in Arkansas.† Most Terminal Island families were sent

---

† Today, according to Roger Daniels in *Concentration Camps USA*, most agree that the relocation centers were nothing more than benign concentration camps. Members of the Japanese-American West Cost minority were confined in them for periods of up to four years and then resettled outside the coastal zone. Thus thousands of American citizens were subjected to long-term forcible detention without having been charged with any offense and without any

to Manzanar in the Owens Valley area of Central California. Local newspapers reported that $300,000 was deposited with the court to compensate property owners. However, the California Alien Land Law of 1913 prevented Asian immigrants from owning land. The Japanese families, who rented their small wooden homes from canning companies and other owners, received no compensation for lost jobs, property, homes and freedom until the fight for reparations made itself visible in the 1980s.

With World War II over, Japanese families returning to Fish Harbor found most of the land they once lived on gone, incorporated into Roosevelt Navy Base. However, they found the resentment among the harbor community against Japanese still there. Non-union fishing boat owners flatly refused to hire any of the Japanese as fishermen. Eventually, when some of the former Fish Harbor residents could afford their own vessels, they were again able to earn their living as fishermen. Most, however, relocated and assimilated quite well. C. Robert Ryono writes that former Fish Harbor residents now live in Florida, Pennsylvania, New York, Minnesota, Illinois, Wisconsin and Rhode Island. However, the deep bonds of the community remain and many come back yearly to attend the Japanese Terminal Island reunion. Presently the group, Terminal Islanders, is raising funds for a memorial of the land and the many Japanese families who made their life at Fish Harbor.††

pretense of due process of law. The Supreme Court, despite the constitutional implications of the relocation program, persistently refused to interpose its authority, apparently because it hesitated to directly challenge the "military necessity" argument. In the process, the Supreme Court created a military-necessity constitutional argument potentially dangerous for the future of American liberty.

†† For information on how to reach the "Terminal Islanders" contact Long Beach Public Library.

W ater sports have long been popular along the Long Beach shore. The city was the center of aquatic activities during both the 1933 and 1988 Olympics. Water skiing, boat racing, rowing, and canoeing can still be enjoyed in the bays. However, many people do not know that Long Beach was once known as the "Waikiki of California" and home to the sport of surfing.

Looking around Long Beach today, it is hard to envision the "long beach" that gave the city its name. Seven miles of sand stretching towards Orange County was the reason that Long Beach was called the "Queen of the Beaches." The various breakwaters put in to build the harbor helped destroy the waves that once crashed along the shore. But there was a time when they did, and it was here in Long Beach that one of the first demonstrations of the Hawaiian sport of surf riding took place.

Breakwater, 1958 L.B.P.L.

Long Beach, the Waikiki of California

In April 1910, W.P. Wheeler of Monroe, Michigan arrived in Long Beach to spend some time. He wintered in Hawaii and was impressed with the surfboats used there. He told the *Long Beach Press* that some enterprising person in Long Beach should use surfboats like those in Honolulu. Wheeler, a beach bum at heart, had visited many seaside resorts. He remarked that Long Beach was the only beach he could compare with Waikiki. It was shallow and long, and the surf rolled in exactly as it did in Hawaii.

At Waikiki, one could rent the surfboats for twenty-five cents a day. However the sport was so popular that many owned their own crafts. The boats ranged from 8 to 14 feet long, were flat and narrow and no more than 18 inches across and 4 inches deep. Each surfboat held from one to four people. Most of the riders in the Waikiki surf stood up in the boats, using a long narrow paddle to keep upright. The "surfer" then swam or paddled the craft through the surf and waited for a big wave, getting on the crest of the wave, just as it was breaking, and paddling away until the momentum of the surf brought him to shore.

Wheeler told the paper he saw surfboats carried over 1,000 feet until they were hurled on the beach. He said it was a great sport for those who knew what they were doing, such as the Hawaiians. Novices, however, had to be prepared for a mouthful of water, until they perfected their skills.

Some enterprising Long Beach visitors, Charles Allbright and A.J. Stout, did take up Wheeler's idea of surf riding, and on September 3, 1911 saved the lives of two men with the help of their Hawaiian surfboards. The *Daily Telegram* reported it was one of the most novel rescues ever pulled off in the surf at Long Beach.

Allbright, a chauffeur for a Pittsburgh doctor, was staying at the Long Beach luxury hotel, the Virginia, along with Stout who was the manager of the Seaside Hotel at Waikiki. The two became friends in Honolulu and brought Hawaiian surfboards to the mainland to try them out in Southern California waters. They were quite a hit along the beach, attracting a crowd whenever they went out with their surfboards. Their boards were not like the multi-person surfboats described by Wheeler, but were geared to individual riders. People were amazed that Allbright and Stout stood on the surfboards and coasted rapidly ashore. It was while they were out in the breakers enjoying themselves that the two surfers became aware of the struggles of two drowning men.

Paul Rowan, a strong swimmer, was out beyond the breakers when he heard a cry for help. The unidentified tourist gurgled "For God's sake, help me! I have a wife on shore,"[1] then grabbed Rowan and held him as he went under. When Rowan told the man to relax a bit, the drowning man grabbed harder and forced Rowan beneath the water. It was at this point that Allbright and Stout became aware of the situation and went to help.

The newspaper reported it was the peculiar design of the Hawaiian surfboards that was responsible for the effective rescues. The boards, made of beautifully grained Hawaiian koa wood, were six feet long, three inches thick, eighteen inches wide and capable of carrying the weight of two men. The fact that both Allbright and Stout were experienced surfers helped with saving the lives of the drowning victim.

Local lifeguards who witnessed the event, decided they needed these Hawaiian surfboards to help them with similar rescues. It appeared as if surfing had arrived on the Southern California coast.

Duke Kahanamoku

In July 1913, a true Hawaiian surfer, Duke Kahanamoku, rode the surf in Long Beach. The famous swimmer and 1912 Olympic champion was in Southern California to compete in a swim meet at the Los Angeles Athletic Club. The Duke, as Kahanamoku was nicknamed, narrowly beat a Long Beach boy, Pete Lenz, who invited the Hawaiian to come and visit the "Queen of the Beaches."

Kahanamoku and six other Hawaiians readily agreed, for they heard the beach at Long Beach rivaled that of Waikiki. Being true surfers, they rarely went anywhere near the ocean without proper surf gear, and when they saw the breakers at Long Beach, they grabbed their surfboards and jumped right in. The Duke and his teammates spontaneously gave a thrilling exhibition of surfboard riding before a crowd of thousands. In fact, so successful was the Hawaiians' demonstration of this new sport, that the people at the Pike seriously considered staging frequent surfboard riding exhibitions. They felt surf riding would draw many to the beach and the amusement area.

It was Kahanamoku's Southland visit that inspired young surf riders to pursue the sport. By June 1914, when neighboring Huntington Beach Pier was dedicated, Hawaiian-born surfer George Freeth was invited to demonstrate his skills on a board during opening day ceremonies.

One of Long Beach's first surfers was Haig Prieste, who won an Olympic diving medal at the 1920 Olympics. At the games, he met fellow Olympian Duke Kahanamoku and accepted an invitation to visit him in Hawaii. Intending to be away only three weeks, Prieste ended up staying three months, partly so he could learn to surf as well as the Islanders. Prieste was amazed that the Hawaiian surfers were able to ride for three-quarters of a mile, gathering speeds up to thirty-five miles per hour. Their ability to pilot their surfboards for great distances in a zigzag course fascinated the champion diver. Prieste quickly figured out that it was very important to position the board diagonally at the correct angle, just at the right moment to avoid being dumped on the coral reefs below. Prieste perfected his surf riding skills by spending eight to ten hours a day in the water. His moment of glory came when he was able to astonish the Hawaiians by riding a board while standing on his hands. Prieste told reporters that surfing was the greatest sport in the world.

Again, in July 1922, Duke Kahanamoku, who won Olympic fame in the 1920 swimming events, returned to the surf in Long Beach. Surfing was now a popular pastime of local youths who were frequently bothered by bathers who refused to get out of their way. Southern California surfing was also taking on a persona of its own in the development of new surfboards, different than those used in Hawaii. Not all beaches were like the one in Long Beach, the Waikiki of California, which responded well to the large, heavy, Hawaiian model board. Beach breaks were different and affected by weather changes far out to sea. Lighter and smaller boards were developed to meet the challenges of these varying wave shapes and sizes.

Surfing competition, 1938 H.S.L.B

Duke Kahanamoku, sponsored by the Outrigger Club of Honolulu, arrived on the mainland to give public exhibitions of his swimming skills. Holding every world swimming honor in his class, he was a hero to be emulated, not only in swimming but in his native Hawaiian sport of surfing as well. On July 31, 1922, the Duke surfed in front of the Hotel Virginia before a crowd of 5,000. It was not a tremendous day for breakers, but local surfers held their own against the Duke because of the boards they developed for Southern California waters.

Kahanamoku brought a long, wide, heavy, pointed Hawaiian surfboard. Ten of the ordinary surfboards seen along the local beach would fit into Duke's. Maybe it was this large Hawaiian board that handicapped Kahanamoku in the Long Beach surf, for he was not able to catch as many waves as the local lads.

By September 1922, the Duke shook the dust of Hawaii from his feet and made the Los Angeles area his home. He was going to be a movie star. He proved himself a real hero, more than just the celluloid variety. In June 1925 he rescued eight passengers from a sinking yacht off Newport Beach. Thanks to Kahanamoku, surfing grew in popularity. By 1928, the Corona Del Mar Surfboard Club, which claimed to be the largest organization of its kind in the world, held a surf riding tournament at Corona Del Mar in Newport Beach. It featured not only Duke Kahanamoku, but popular local riders such as Tom Blake of Redondo Beach, Gerard & Art Vultee of the Los Angeles Athletic Club and Clyde Swedson of the Hollywood Athletic Club. It was an exciting contest. A 400-pound mackerel shark cruising the bay caused the contestants to face the challenge of avoiding the shark while still catching the surf.

Surfing became so popular that in the summer of 1933 Long Beach adopted City Ordinance No. C-1195, restricting surfboard riders to certain areas of the beach. Surfers were fined $500 and put in jail for six months if they violated the law. The restrictions did not help Phyllis Hines, however, when on July 5, 1937 she was killed when her surfboard jabbed her in the stomach. It was the first surfboard fatality on record.

1938 Surfing competition H.S.L.B.

National Surfing and Paddleboard Competition

A little-known fact of surf history is that Long Beach was host to the first National Surfing and Paddleboard championships, the first countrywide title event ever held in the surfing world. On Sunday, November 13, 1938, more than 150 of America's finest surfers competed for the mammoth silver trophy presented to the winning team and for the gold trophies given to individual winners.

The event, sponsored jointly by the Long Beach Junior Chamber of Commerce and the Long Beach Amusement League, started with a half-mile paddleboard race through the surf. Women as well as men competed. It was the surfing championships, however, that were broadcast live over radio station KFOX that attracted most of the attention. Twenty thousand people crowded onto Rainbow and Silver Spray piers, and the beach in front of the Pike to view the competition.

Preston Peterson and Mary Ann Hawkins, of the Del Mar Surfing Club won the national paddleboard division, but lack of heavy surf postponed the surfing competition until December 11, 1938. The surfers, however, could not disappoint the crowd who came to see them perform and the radio audience who were listening. A trial open surfing event was held with John Olsen of Long Beach winning the competition, James McGrew of Beverly Hills placing second and Denny Watson of Venice placing third.

1938 Surfing Competition in Long Beach H.S.L.B.

On a cold December 11,1938, 40,000 onlookers watched sixty-five surfers compete in team and individual competitions. The Santa Ana Band led the participants, whose boards ranged in length from eleven to eighteen feet, to the

1939 Surf competition in Long Beach H.S.L.B.

edge of the surf between Rainbow and Silver Spray piers where the water temperature was fifty-two degrees.   Newsreel, magazine and newspaper photographers were there taking pictures of the event.

It was the Manhattan Surfing Club that won the forty-four inch silver perpetual team cup. The Venice Surfing Club placed second, Santa Monica third, Palos Verdes Surfriders Club fourth, and the Del Mar Club fifth. The open surfing championship was won by Arthur Horner of Venice, with Jim Kerwin of

John Olsen winner, 1939 H.S.L.B.

Manhattan Beach coming in second, and Don Campbell, also of Manhattan Beach, third. Medals were given to Chuck Allen, Palos Verdes, fourth place; Tom Ehlers, Manhattan Beach, fifth place; Kenneth Beck, Venice, sixth; Bob Reinhard and John Lind of Long Beach, seventh and eighth.

So successful was this first national surfing championship, that Long Beach vowed to make it an annual event. On December 3, 1939 the second annual national surfing contest was held off Rainbow Pier. Fog hampered viewers, but not the judges. The Hermosa Beach Surfing Club, followed by Manhattan Beach, Venice and Long Beach won the three-man team event. Gene Smith, member of the Hawaiian Surfing Club, which traveled all the way to Long Beach for this competition, competed alone against the other teams after his two teammates, A.C. Spohler and Jack May, withdrew because of the weather conditions. Amazingly, Smith finished fifth against the heavy odds. Individual surfing honors went to Long Beach Surfing Club members John Olsen, who finished first, Alvin Bixler, second, and Bob Reinhard, fourth. Gene Smith of Hawaii came in third.

1939 Surfing championship H.S.L.B.

This was the last national surf contest held in Long Beach. World War II broke out in Europe and soon the United States was involved. The harbor breakwater was completed in the 1940s and the U.S. Navy made Terminal Island its home. After the war, surfers returning from battle found there were rarely waves in Long Beach to ride--the breakwater had seen to that. Maybe once a year surfer-worthy waves would get to Long Beach through a southwest facing gap in the breakwater that stretched from 55th Place to the end of the Alamitos Bay jetty at 72nd Place on the Peninsula. It served as a reminder of how great the surf once was. When the Navy shut down its operations in Long Beach in 1998, surf enthusiasts and the Surfrider Foundation asked for the removal of the breakwater to bring back the waves. Only the future will reveal how successful they are.

Beach Culture

In 1911, at the same time Allbright and Stout were demonstrating their skills on the Hawaiian surfboards, a new beach fad was developing--sunglasses.

Wearing "smoked glasses" became de rigueur at Long Beach's Hotel Virginia. Anyone who wanted to appear in vogue had the latest eyewear perched on their nose. The glare of the sun on the sand and water was a problem for beachgoers for some time. As a result, smoked glasses, formerly worn only by the blind, were developed. The "blinders" as some people called them came in two colors--red and blue. The problem was that those who wore the blue always appeared to have a gloomy expression, while those attired in red always saw things in that color.

Bathing attire at Long Beach, 1920s H.S.L.B.

By 1920, beach attire was a major problem for Long Beach officials. Fashions in bathing suits were becoming more and more shocking, almost approaching nudity. Many people avoided the beach because of the unseemly costumes and undesirable people who wore them. "Modern" women, tired of the old skirts, were buying men's bathing suits. In fact, one merchant said he sold fifteen men's suits to women to every one made for a woman.

In May 1920, Long Beach Public Safety Commissioner, William M. Peek, rushed through an ordinance stating that bathing suits could not be too tight, must have skirts and at least the rudiments of sleeves. Bathers not in the water had to wear cloaks over their suits. Peek paid a visit to Catalina Island and found that women bathers at Avalon had to wear stockings. Peek said that the ordinance he was drafting would not be as extreme. Its final form read:

> No person shall appear in or upon any highway or other public place, upon the sand or beach along or near the shore of the Pacific Ocean, or in the Pacific Ocean, in the city of Long Beach, clothed in a bathing suit which does not completely conceal from view all the trunk of the body of such person and each leg from the hip joint to a peripheric line one-third of the way to the knee joint, except that the chest and back between the shoulders to a peripheric line even with the upper parts of the armpits may be exposed to view, and without such bathing suit having attached thereto a skirt made of the same kind of material as the bathing suit, completely surrounding the person and hanging loosely from the peripheric line at the waist to the bottom of such bathing suit.[2]

There was equality between the sexes in this law. The ordinance mandated that men as well as women had to wear skirts. Violation of the bathing suit ordinance was punishable by six months imprisonment, a fine of $500, or both. It applied to all persons over six years of age including lifeguards. Peek went on to add:

> Six-foot Apollos garbed in one-piece bathing garments intended for 14-year old boys will not be permitted to pace the strand. If there is no other way to compel observance, they will be discharged from the city force. [3]

This is Jantzen Week
from Maine to Waikiki!

Daily Telegram ad 7/7/1922

There was a new bathing suit design that Commissioner Peek approved--one that was non-sinkable. It was made buoyant by inserting a small rubber tube into the fabric. It was guaranteed to be comfortable for the wearer and keep him or her above water. Peek hoped the patent owners, the Battelle's, would set up their manufacturing plant in Long Beach.

Despite restrictions on what could be worn in the water, surfing grew in popularity and by 1922 the romantic image of the surfer was born. Ads appeared featuring surfboards and surfing, Jantzen swim-suits were one of the first companies to portray both men and women (without skirted suits) challenging the waves on their boards. Despite the modern fashions, Long Beach's bathing suit regulations remained on the books into the early 1930s.

In 1932, it appeared as if the wearing of swimming trunks in Long Beach was given the okay when a jury acquitted two young men charged with wearing suits which were "too abbreviated." However, a revised bathing suit ordinance was quickly adopted stating that suits could not be rolled down to the waist or be made of translucent materials. Thirty arrests soon followed.

In 1962, surf wear changed once more due to the efforts of one Long Beach company. The Doris Moore of California clothing manufacturer developed the "Hang Ten" surf wear line to meet the needs of the growing surf market. Working on the recommendations of surfer Duke Boyd, Doris Moore produced a few sample swim trunks. From personal experience, Boyd knew that surfers needed trunks longer than those for swimming with a wide and strong waistband. Moore also developed a special Velcro closure so that buttons, which could pull off, and zippers, which foul up in the sand, were not needed. Boyd showed the new trunks to other surfers and returned in two weeks with orders for 500 pairs. By 1964 more than 70,000 pairs Hang Ten trunks had been sold.

170

NOTES & BIBLIOGRAPHY

INTRODUCTION
Notes:

[1] Jefferson, Thomas, *Life and Selected Writings of Thomas Jefferson*, New York, Modern Library, 1998, p. 532.

Bibliography:

Berner, Loretta. "Looking back at Long Beach: a new name, a new company, and railroad troubles." *Long Beach Review*, October 1986. p. 13.

CHAPTER 1 - Sea Serpents & Other Oddities
Notes:

[1] Bandini, Ralph. *Tight Lines*. Los Angeles, Tight Lines Publishers, 1932, p.50-55.

[2] "Ol' Clemente Clem back in news again." *Press-Telegram*, 5 June 1953, B1:5.

[3] "Sea monster panics Pike." *Long Beach Independent*, 1 April 1949, A1:1.

[4] "Sub torpedo saves city from sea monster." *Long Beach Independent*, 1 April 1949, A7:1.

[5] "Ghost fish is puzzler for boatmen." *Long Beach Press*, 3 September 1915, 2:1.

Bibliography:

"Abalone." *The New Funk & Wagnalls Illustrated Wildlife Encyclopedia*. New York, Funk & Wagnalls, 1980.

"Abalone holds diver in ocean." *Long Beach Press*, 21 July 1911, 10:4.

"Angler boats six-foot, 22-pound sea oddity." *Press-Telegram*, 9 September 1957, B2-5.

"Antczak, John. "Octopus yanks plug from tank, found dead." *Press-Telegram*, 12 April 1994, B2-1.

"Attacked by an octopus near Locust." *Long Beach Press*, 5 August 1907, 1:7.

"Big sea turtle dies; potato diet." *Long Beach Press*, 17 May 1921, 14:6.

Canto, Minerva. "It really was wet: El Niño rain season tally was twice average year's." *Press-Telegram*, 30 June 1998, 1:1.

Cashman, Katherine. "Krakatau." *World Book Encyclopedia*. Chicago, World Book, 1997, v.11, pg. 386.

Collins, Jeff "Tropical whale washes ashore in Newport Beach". *Orange County Register*, 19 February 1998, Metro 1:7.

Copley International Corporation. *Water quality and saltwater habitats of Long Beach*. La Jolla, Author, 1974.

Copley International Corporation. *Zoological survey City of Long Beach*. La Jolla, Author, 1974.

"Death toll from El Niño put at 23,000." *Orange County Register*, 13 February 1999, 11:1.

"Devilfish catch man in bathing." *Long Beach Press*, 10 October 1911, 3:4.

"Eerie sound over harbor baffles city." *Press-Telegram*, 28 December 1961, B1-4.

Fisher, Eugene I. "Pioneer tales of early days in Long Beach as related by old-timers." *Long Beach Press*, 31 January 1914, 12:4.

"Freakish fish caught in surf near harbor." *Press-Telegram*, 2 July 1935, B1-4.

Gilbertas, Bernadette. "Up from the sand." *International Wildlife*, September-October 1998, p.30.

Gordon David G. "Sea Monsters in the Pacific?" *Readers Digest*, January 1988, v.132, no. 789, p. 21.

Heuvelmans, Bernard. *In the Wake of the Sea-serpents*. New York, Hill and Wang, 1968.

"Is it a Vesuvius, or a gopher-hole in the smoking flank of Mount Hoar?" *Los Angeles Times*, 21 September 1883, 2:2.

"The Javanese calamity." *Los Angeles Times*, 7 September 1883, 2:1.

Koch, Margaret. "Monsters of the deep came ashore from the bay." *Santa Cruz Sentinel*, 4 Jan. 1989, D-2.

"Leviathan may be sea serpent or submarine." *Long Beach Press*, 30 December 1911, 3:7.

Long Beach. City Planning Commission. *Master Environmental Inventory*. Long Beach, Author, 1978.

"Mount Hoar and its alleged smoking volcano." *Los Angeles Times*, 16 September 1883, 2:2.

"Octopus." *Encyclopedia of the Animal World*. Syndey, Australia, Bay Books. 1977.

"Odd things washing up on beaches." *Press-Telegram*, 29 July 1955 B1-4.

"Orange County: monster washed ashore." *Los Angeles Times*, 23 February 1901, 12:2.

"Peculiar denizen of deep disports in surf in front of bathhouse." *Daily Telegram*, 11 March 1907, 1:5.

Pritchard, Peter. *Encyclopedia of turtles*. Neptune, NJ., T.F.H., 1979.

"A puzzle unlocked: fishy story." *The Economist*, 29 August 1992, v.324, no.7774, p.76.

Randell, David H. "Geology of the City of Long Beach, California, United States of America." *Bulletin of the Association of Engineering Geologists*, XX, no.1, February 1983.

"Real live sea serpent seen at fishing banks." *Daily Telegram*, 17 February 1909, 1:7.

"Risk arms to gather beautiful abalone: shell business here worth $200,000 per year." *Long Beach Press Magazine*, 17 September 1922, 4:1.

Roberts, William C. "California's Nessie: pondering the possibility that pre-historic creatures survive in the Pacific." *Skin Diver*, November 1989, v. 38, no. 11, p.154.

Rosenthal, E. Jane. "The Bulrush Canyon project: excavations at Bulrush Canyon Site and Camp Cactus Road site, Santa Catalina Island." *Pacific Coast Archaeological Society Quarterly*, April & July 1988, v.24, nos. 2&3, p.1-120.

Rowe, Jeff. "Lobster haul huge, but there's a catch." *Orange County Register*, 9 October 1997, A1-6.

"Statistics." *The Economist*, 28 November 1998, p. 87.

"This turtle a monster: twenty feet long and weighs about three thousand pounds." *Los Angeles Times*, 29 July 1907, 16:2.

"Tidal wave tale is cause of unusual flurry." *Long Beach Press*, 22 May 1919, 14:1.

Tyson, Peter. "High-tech help for ancient turtles." *MIT's Technology Review*. November-December 1997, v.100, no. 8, p.54.

Williams, Vera. "Hills rise from depths of Pacific." *Press-Telegram*, 2 October 1955, C2-2.

Williams, Vera. "Hundred kinds of fish abound." *Press-Telegram*, 16 October 1955, C2-2.

CHAPTER 2 - Otter Hunting
Bibliography:
"Home for lepers on an island: San Miguel proposed as the home for them -- Cabrillo and his armor of gold buried there." *Evening Tribune*, 28 May 1904.

"Islands of the sea." *Los Angeles Times*, 1 January 1895.

"The lone woman of San Nicolas." *Los Angeles Times*, 8 January 1899, 11:1.

Manville, Rhonda Parks. "Otters don't look cute to fishermen." *Press-Telegram*, 26 June 1998, A16:1.

O'Dell, Scott. *Island of the Blue Dolphins*. Boston, Houghton Mifflin, 1960.

O'Dell, Scott. *Zia*. New York, Dell, 1976.

Ogden, Adele. *The California Sea Otter Trade, 1784-1848*. Berkeley, University of California Press, 1941.

"Otter hunting: the sharp shooters of the Santa Barbara channel." *Los Angeles Times*, 11 November 1883, 4:4.

"San Miguel's skeleton secret: Long Beach boatman tells of ghastly discovery on lonely island." *Long Beach Press*, 30 October 1915, 1:1.

"Sea Otters". *The New International Wildlife Encyclopedia*. Milwaukee, Purnell Reference Books, 1980, v. 15, p. 2076.

Stevens, William K. "Ominous otter ouster." *Orange County Register*, 16 February 1999, 10:1.

CHAPTER 3 - Whale Tales
Notes:
[1] "Flying in Navy blimp, Capt. Loop tests patent blow devil whale lance." *Daily Telegram*, 19 August 1921, 17:1.

Bibliography:
"Airplane whale hunting, invented by L.B. captain, practiced by naval force." *Daily Telegram*, 31 July 1922, 9:1.

"Albino dolphin seen off coast." *Long Beach Press*, 14 October 1915, 1:4.

"Black fish says old whaler." *Long Beach Press*, 9 January 1914, 1:1.

"Blimp is being made for new sport of harpooning whales." *Daily Telegram,* 26 July 1920, 9:1.

"Bones of the whale caught here recently are about to be cured and ready for mounting." *Los Angeles Times,* 6 June 1897, 31:2.

"Decide on plans for library; to be 60 x 100, two-story and basement including whale." *Long Beach Press,* 28 March 1908, 1:5.

"Elephant cemetery? Big discovery made by 3 Lakewood boys." *Press-Telegram,* 12 June 1960, A1-2.

"Embalming of giant whale taken here." *Long Beach Press,* 29 March 1916, 6:4.

"Gas-filled harpoon is latest invention for killing whales." *Press-Telegram,* 25 January 1925, 3:10:2.

"L.A. Museum adopts whale." *Independent Press-Telegram,* 26 July 1974, B1-4.

Lilley, Ray. "Evidence of illegal whale trade found in Asia." *Orange County Register,* 12 May 1998, A8:2.

"Loop gets leviathan, feat beats world's record." *Long Beach Press,* 4 January 1912, 1:5.

"Minnie, faded star of lagoon, primps for mammoth return." *Press-Telegram,* 1 February 1954, B2-2.

Nickerson, Colin. "Inuit, environmentalists at odds over whale hunt." *Orange County Register,* 28 July 1998, 11:3.

"Porpoise hide as substitute to oust rubber." *Long Beach Press,* 8 June 1916, 12:4

"Refining machine on barge J.D. Loop." *Long Beach Press,* 8 January 1912, 6:5.

"Sightseers flock to see giant leviathan." *Long Beach Press,* 6 January 1912, 10:1.

"Strange sea creatures sighted." *Long Beach Press,* 8 January 1914, 1:3.

"Two whales shot by Captain Loop." *Long Beach Press,* 7 December 1911, 3:1.

Weeks, George. "Minnie the Whale rattles again: bones not an elephant's." *Press-Telegram,* 16 June 1960, B1-6.

"Whale must stay." *Evening Tribune,* 13 January 1904, 1:2.

"Whale steaks pronounced delicious." *Long Beach Press,* 21 November 1916, 13:1.

CHAPTER 4 - Seal Tales

Notes:

1 "Park lagoon favored as home for seals." *Press-Telegram*, 26 March 1925, 13:3.

Bibliography:

"Baby seal adopts L.B. lads." *Press-Telegram*, 9 April 1950, B1:2.

Cox, John D. "Sea lion killings get U.S. approval." *Orange County Register*, 13 February 1999, 6:1.

"Governor signs bill protecting seals near city." *Press-Telegram*, 26 May 1925, 12:7.

Haines, Audrey B. "Seals are born clowns." *Independent Press-Telegram*, 21 June 1959, Southland Magazine:7.

"Lonesome seal pays visit to L.B. apartment." *Press-Telegram*, 11 January 1955, B1:2.

Masciola, Carol. "Sea lions take over Newport waters." *Orange County Register*, 9 July 1998, 1:1.

"Pet seal sold to circus." *Daily Telegram*, 2 October 1906, 1:4.

"Seals interest visitors at Belmont Shore Place; seal farm effort failed." *Daily Telegram*, 23 July 1922, D2-1.

"Seals may be shipped to Lake Elsinore." *Press-Telegram*, 21 March 1925, 9:8.

"Strange game: lassoing seals in the caverns of Santa Cruz Island." *Los Angeles Times* 9 July 1899, 8:1.

Zinser, Ben. "Lost Lake Elsinore returns; Railroad Canyon waters flood back into dry bed." *Independent Press-Telegram*, 13 April 1958, A1-1.

CHAPTER 5 - Sharks

Bibliography:

CAP flies shark patrol off shore." *Press-Telegram*, 28 June 1959, A5-1.

"Council seeking shark safeguard for L.B. waters." *Press-Telegram*, 24 June 1959, B1-2.

"First shark of man-eating kind ever seen in these waters captured today. " *Daily Telegram*, 13 February 1908, 1:5.

"A fish story." *Los Angeles Times*, 28 August 1883, 4:5.

"Hundreds flee as shark seen: swimmers ordered out of Seal Beach surf." *Press-Telegram*, 20 July 1959, B1-4.

McCauley, Jim. "Shark off La Jolla gulps and likes Navy repellent." *Press-Telegram*, 21 June 1959, A1-2.

"Man-eater shark leaps onto ship." *Long Beach Press*, 21 September 1912, 9:4.

"Million-to-one odds against shark attack." *Press-Telegram*, 28 June 1959, A1-1.

Resnik, Bert. "L.B. men battle 20-foot shark one hour off local beach." *Press-Telegram*, 20 November 1955, A1-2.

"Shark menace grows." *Press-Telegram*, 5 June 1959, B2-1.

"Shark menace seen increasing." *Press-Telegram*, 17 June 1959, A17-1.

"Shark off L.B. shore frightens thousands." *Press-Telegram*, 22 June 1959, B1-2.

"Shark pack thwarts channel swimmer." *Press-Telegram*, 27 June 1959, B1-2.

"Sharks". *World Book Encyclopedia*. Chicago, World Book, Inc., 1997.

"Twelve foot shark gives cops bad scare." *Daily Telegram*, 24 July 1913, 1:4.

"2 missing while on shark hunt." *Press-Telegram*, 29 June 1959, B1-3.

"Watch found in shark stomach." *Independent Press-Telegram*, 24 June 1959, B2-1.

"Watch in shark just a hoax, crewman says." *Press-Telegram*, 1 July 1959, B1-8.

Wells, Bob. "Skin divers doubt shark peril: don't swim off hastily, just look angry." *Press-Telegram*, 25 June 1959, B2-1.

"Wife sees shark kill skin-diver at La Jolla." *Press-Telegram*, 15 June 1959, A1-3.

CHAPTER 6 - Sea Adventures
Bibliography:

"Sailor `boy' was a girl." *Evening Tribune*, 6 January 1906, 1:3

"Sea venture of Long Beach wanderer." *Long Beach Press*, 28 September 1916, 2:1.

"She wanted to be a sailor." *Evening Tribune*, 27 September 1905, 1:1.

"Wants to be a boy: Bessie Barclay has a longing to wear trousers." *Evening Tribune*, 4 January 1904, 1:1.

PART 2 - INTRODUCTION
Bibliography:

"Camel tooth dug up near this city." *Long Beach Press*, 20 June 1914, 1:5.

"Explorers dig for ancient city under Los Angeles site." *Press-Telegram*, 29 January 1934, A3:5.

"Fossil find of ancient ship is recalled." *Long Beach Press*, 17 July 1914, 1:6.

CHAPTER 7 - The Long Beach Earthquake and the Viking Ship
Bibliography:

Cusler, Clive. *Inca Gold*. New York, Simon & Schuster, 1994.

Ewers, Retta, "Lost Galleon of the Desert." *Press-Telegram*, 5 May 1963, Southland: 50.

Pepper, Choral. *Desert Lore of Southern California*. San Diego, Sunbelt Publications, 1994. p.53-56.

"Search for ancient ship fruitless." *Press-Telegram*, 21 Apr. 1929, C1-4.

CHAPTER 8 - Long Beach man builds his own Noah's Ark
Bibliography:

"Lewis gets new ark for trip to Negro state." *Daily Telegram*, 13 December 1922, 11:2.

"Lewis ark sails February 3 to Liberia on Sho'nuf boat." *Daily Telegram*, 30 January 1923, 14:3.

"More trouble for colored clergyman and his freak ark." *Daily Telegram*, 31 January 1921, 16:11.

"Negro parson's ark meets disaster in being launched." *Daily Telegram*, 11 October 1919, 4:1.

"Negroes have faith in ark launching." *Daily Telegram*, 4 May 1921, 9:1.

CHAPTER 9 - Manila Galleons & Spanish Treasure
Bibliography:

Gibbs, James A. *Shipwrecks of the Pacific Coast*. Portland, Oregon, Binfords & Mort, 1962.

Parrish, Michael. *Treasure Hunters*. Los Angeles, November 1983, 124.

Penfield, Thomas. *A Guide to Treasure in California.* Conroe, Texas, True Treasure Library, 1972.

Potter, John S. *The Treasure Diver's Guide.* New York, Doubleday, 1960.

CHAPTER 10 - Pirates & Hidden Treasure
Bibliography:

Booth, P.H. "The Smugglers of Portuguese Bend." *Independent Press-Telegram*, 24 February 1963, Southland Magazine:8.

"Catalina's mines: an old-time mining rush with its usual grand finale." *Los Angeles Times*, 3 December 1899, p.21:1.

"Copper spike is believed relic Spanish galleon." *Long Beach Press*, 24 February 1913, 1:2.

Crump, Spencer. "Hippolyte was here! Long Beach sands hide pirate loot?" *Independent Press-Telegram*, 4 May 1952, B1-2.

Dunlevy, Bill. "Diver dies marking old ship wreck." *Press-Telegram*, 4 June 1960, A1-4.

"Everybody in Alamitos taking gold cure." *Daily Telegram*, 7 December 1906, 1:6.

"Four fail to locate pirate loot." *Press-Telegram*, 27 April 1952, A10-6.

"Gold in the sand near Alamitos Bay." *Long Beach Press*, 19 October 1905, 1:7.

Hazelleaf, Robert. "Sunken treasure off the west coast." *Independent Press-Telegram*, 13 March 1960, Southland Magazine:7.

"Human bones in mahogany case: ghastly find of fishermen on Deadman's Island." *Daily Telegram*, 6 July 1906, 4:2.

Hull, Edna M. "The treasures of Catalina." *Independent Press-Telegram*, 26 April 1959, Southland Magazine: .9.

"Losers help police dig buried loot at Naples." *Press-Telegram*, 3 August 1922, B1-1.

"Park steam shovel digs up skeleton of ancient sea captain." *Press-Telegram*, 1 November 1924, 13:6.

"Santa Catalina: the stone relics of an extinct race." *Los Angeles Times*, 13 January 1893.

CHAPTER 11 Treasure & Gambling Ships

Bibliography:

"Chicago acts barred from record." *Press-Telegram*, 2 April 1931, B1-1.

"Cornero loses in attempt to halt action." *Press-Telegram*, 11 August 1939, A1-2.

"Cornero resists effort to board palatial Rex." *Press-Telegram*, 2 August 1939.

"Court ruling to abate gaming ships." *Press-Telegram*, 18 October 1939, B1-8.

"Gang may have operated locally: Long Beach crimes may be traced to mystery burial bandits." *Press-Telegram*, 27 March 1930, A1-4.

"Gangsters are given limit in penalty." *Press-Telegram*, 16 March 1932, A1-1.

Grobaty, Tim. "There was action aplenty just offshore." *Press-Telegram*, 22 April 1988, D1-2.

"Officer shot in spine by gangsters." *Press-Telegram*, 22 December 1930, A1-1.

"Six extra men posted at building; eleventh-hour attempt to free prisoners is feared by State. *Press-Telegram*, 17 April 1931, A1-2.

"Suspects released; cleared of shooting charge." *Press-Telegram*, 10 April 1931, A1-1.

"$3000 on gambling boat recovered by ocean divers." *Press-Telegram*, 5 September 1930, B1-5.

CHAPTER 12 - The Cage Submarine

Notes:

[1] "Ad." *Daily Telegram*, 7 March 1913, A1-3.

[2] "The Cage six-cycle, three-phase silent engine." *Daily Telegram*, 7 April 1914, 1:4.

Bibliography:

"Belated report of submarine boat agent. *Daily Telegram*. 6 January 1915, 5:3.

"Cage submarine being made ready for submergence test." *Daily Telegram*, 9 June 1913, 1:4.

Crossman, E.C. "Gas engine drive for submerged submarines: a California experiment which aims to supplant the storage battery." *Scientific American*, 25 August 1917, v. 117, no. 8, p.132.

Edholm, Charlton Lawrence. "Thirty-six hours under water: a submarine propelled by gasoline engines while submerged." *Scientific American*, 21 June 1913, v. 108, no. 25, p. 556.

"Is German government using Cage submarine?" *Daily Telegram*, 30 August 1917, 4:1.

"Navy may test submarine boat, local invention." *Press-Telegram*, 15 August 1924, 4:3.

"New submarine takes shape in steel." *Long Beach Press*, 18 November 1911, 12:4.

"Shifting ballast causes mishap to new Cage submarine." *Daily Telegram*, 18 January 1913, 1:6.

"Submarine Boat work deferred: A.R. Neff reads Daniels' letter at L.A. Sub. meeting." *Daily Telegram*, 7 January 1918, 4:4.

"Submarine breaks world's record for submergence." *Daily Telegram*, 11 June 1913, 1:6.

"Submarine patents again in company hands: local corporation has just received notice of reassignment of claims held by Abner Neff." *Daily Telegram*, 13 August 1918, p.10:7.

"Submarine sold for song: Cage craft bid in by creditor for $400, assuming claims." *Daily Telegram*, 30 December 1913, 4:4.

CHAPTER 13 - Japanese Submarines at the Bottom of the Bay?
Notes:
[1] U.S. Coast Guard. *Letter to Claudine Burnett*. 14 January 1998.

[2] U.S. Dept. of the Navy. Naval Historical Center. *Letter to Claudine Burnett*. 2 March 1998.

Bibliography:
"Army lifts secrecy on 1942 battle." *Press-Telegram*, 29 October 1945, B1-4.

"Effort to find Nip submarine wreckage fails." *Press-Telegram*, 27 September 1947, B1-8.

"Mystery raid! Two waves of planes sweep over city as anti-aircraft guns roar. *Long Beach Independent,* 25 February 1942, A1-1.

Newton, Edsel "Diver trying to salvage Jap sub off Pt. Fermin." *Press-Telegram*, 14 May 1946, B1-6.

Parker, Torrance R. *20,000 jobs under the sea: a history of diving and underwater engineering.* Palos Verdes Peninsula, Sub-Sea Archives, 1997.

"Peacetime patrol duty given noted Coast Guard ship." *Press-Telegram*, 12 August 1945 B1-5.

"Salvage of Jap sub, sunk in '41 near here, denied." *Press-Telegram*, 16 February 1946 B1-6.

"Suspect Nip subs heard in harbor thirteen times." *Press-Telegram*, 20 August 1945, B1-3.

U.S. Army. *The United States Army in World War II.* Washington, D.C., Government Printing Office, 1964, p.87.

Wells, Bob. "Mystery still veiling Japanese submarine sunk off San Pedro." *Independent Press-Telegram*, 19 April 1959, A1-2.

CHAPTER 14- Underwater Dump
Bibliography:

"Children warned: live ammo." *Press-Telegram*, 24 March 1958, B2-1.

McCauley, Jim, "Vast A-dump off L.B." *Press-Telegram*, 27 December 1959, A1-1.

Robbins, Gary, "Inside the depot: mysterious base thrives stocking missiles in post-Cold War era." *Orange County Register*, 23 February 1999, News A10:1.

Shannon, Herb. "Big boom buried in ocean 40 miles from Long Beach." *Independent Press-Telegram*, 13 November 1955, A4-1.

Tuinstra, Rachel. "Toxic plume slowly moving under Naval Weapons Station." *Orange County Register*, 26 February 1999, Metro 1:2.

CHAPTER 15 - The Piers
Bibliography:

"Long Beach citizens excited over prospect of new wharf." *Los Angeles Times*, 14 July 1892, 7:2.

"Long Beach wharf: a big crowd assisted in dedicating it yesterday." *Los Angeles Times*, 28 May 1893, 10:3.

Lowe, Joshua. "Belmont Pier to be Renovated." *Press-Telegram*, 24 June 1999, A2:2.

"Pelican Mike has host of friends and lots of fun by the old pier." *Long Beach Press Magazine*, 25 June 1922, 5:1.

CHAPTER 16 - The Pike
Bibliography:

"The Long Beach `Pike'" *Daily Telegram*, 18 July 1904, 1:4.

"A short trip along the Pike." *Long Beach Press*, 15 March 1905, 6:1.

CHAPTER 17 - Around Alamitos Bay
Bibliography:

"Apartment plea for shore area denied by board, Planning Commission votes Livingston Drive as residence zone." *Press-Telegram*, 21 March 1930, A12-2.

"Belmont Shore showplace of 1920s soon to be razed." *Independent Press-Telegram*, 17 July 1966, B1-2.

"Belmont subdivision lures non-residents." *Press-Telegram*, 16 May 1926, 7:2.

"City of canals was envisioned in 1903." *Press-Telegram*, 17 February 1946, A16-3.

"Father of Alamitos Bay District dies at Harriman Jones Clinic." *Bel-Na-Mos*, 22 June 1939, 1:2.

"Handsome hotel goes up at Naples." *Evening Tribune*, 2 July 1907, 8:5.

"Housing project in Belmont Shore strongly opposed." *Press-Telegram*, 9 June 1942, A4:5.

"Hotel Napoli, vacant quarter century gets new owner." *Press-Telegram*, 9 December 1938 C1-2.

"Naples of America at Alamitos Bay." *Daily Telegram*, 21 July 1905, 3:1.

"Old homesteads are built over for war workers." *Press-Telegram*, 21 February 1943, A2-1.

"Permits given apartments in Belmont." *Press-Telegram*, 12 June 1942, B1-4.

"Plans being remodeled for big Naples Hotel." *Daily Telegram*, 23 August 1907, 1:5.

"Ready to dig Naples canal." *Daily Telegram*, 11 April 1906, 1:3.

"Residential tract of 530 lots near ocean will be developed." *Daily Telegram*, 20 December 1919, 3:1.

"Sale of Belmont Shore property makes new record." *Daily Telegram*, 17 August 1920, 10:1.

CHAPTER 18 - Harbor Hijinks
Notes:
1 "Great gathering of citizens celebrate work on harbor." *Daily Telegram*, 8 January 1906, 1:3.

Bibliography:

"Barbour flees with chest of gold." *Long Beach Press*s, 19 February 1906, 1:8.

"Barbour out of bankruptcy." *Long Beach Press*, 14 January 1907, 1:4.

"Barbour's confidential man has disappeared." *Long Beach Press*, 9 October 1906, 1:5.

"Building of municipal railroad at municipal wharves is authorized." *Long Beach Press*, 11 March 1911, 2:1.

"Canal is open to world." *Long Beach Press*, 15 August 1914, 1:1.

"Contract for ship plant signed today." *Daily Telegram*, 27 February 1907, 1:3.

"Craig shipbuilding firm wants site at Terminal." *Daily Telegram*, 18 May 1906, 1:3.

"Dredger bluffed to a standstill." *Long Beach Press*, 10 August 1906, 1:1.

"Dredger is at work; beginnings of Long Beach harbor are at hand." *Evening Tribune*, 12 December 1905, 1:2.

"Great gathering of citizens celebrate work on harbor." *Daily Telegram*, 8 January 1906, 1:3.

"Harbor opening is ok say captains." *Long Beach Press*, 18 December 1909, 1:3.

"Long Beach celebrates dike's demolition by five minutes' noise." *Long Beach Press*, 10 October 1913, 1:5.

"Long Beach raises $100,000 for Craig ship building plant." *Evening Tribune*, 16 January 1907, 1:1.

"Long Beach to be made an island by great canal." *Long Beach Press*, 4 September 1905, 1:7.

"Municipal docks formally opened to commerce today." *Daily Telegram*, 24 June 1911, 1:3.

"New inner harbor; Burk's land syndicate completes its holdings." *Daily Telegram*, 31 July 1905, 1:3.

184

"Religious sect coming here to bathe in sacred stream." *Long Beach Press*, 17 March 1911, 2:4.

"San Pedro Day." *Los Angeles Times*, 27 April 1899, 10:1.

"San Pedro and Los Angeles join hands by large vote." *Long Beach Press*, 13 August 1909, 2:3.

"San Pedro Harbor: why the engineers again recommend it." *Los Angeles Times*, 10 December 1892, 9:2.

"San Pedro up in arms over attempt to abolish its name." *Long Beach Press*, 14 May 1921, 19:6.

"When Long Beach port was salt slough." *Long Beach Press*, 10 March 1913, 1:2.

"Yacht Lasata is first through big ditch." *Long Beach Press*, 7 September 1914, 2:3.

CHAPTER 19 - Terminal Island & the Fish Trade
Bibliography:

"Canners reported asked to restore Nisei in fishing." *Press-Telegram*, 27 September 1945 B1-3.

Daniels, Roger. *Concentration camps USA: Japanese Americans and World War II*. New York, Holt, Rinehart & Winston, 1972.

"An election is ordered to vote on annexation of Terminal." *Evening Tribune*, 18 July 1905, 1:1.

Executive Order No. 9066, February 19, 1942, in *House Report* No. 2124, 77th Cong., 2d Sess., pp.314-15

"Fish Harbor here unique international settlement." *Press-Telegram*, 13 April 1941, A10: 1.

"For greater Long Beach; Terminal Island and East San Pedro link fortunes with `city that does things'; despite the efforts of jealous San Pedro annexation carries by small majority." *Evening Tribune*, 17 August 1905, 1:3.

"Jap ouster to be completed her Sunday: removal of from 800 to 1000 due in three groups." *Press-Telegram*, 31 March 1942, B1-4.

"Japanese here pledge loyal help: spokesman for 1000 vow they are for American security." *Press-Telegram*, 9 December 1941, B6-5.

"Los Angeles-Long Beach twin port is center of tuna packing industry." *Long Beach Press*, 16 July 1915, 10:2.

"May establish big fish depot; Vancouver man spends day in looking over city's opportunities." *Long Beach Press*, 29 December 1909, 1:3.

"New seafood given world. Canning of tuna becoming immense industry." *Los Angeles Times*, 26 July 1914, II:3:1.

"Poisonous reptiles infest West Long Beach, school children organize killing brigades after school hours and kill 50 a day." *Long Beach Press*, 28 April 1908, 1:3.

"Raid staged on Terminal Island alien Japanese." *Press-Telegram*, 4 February 1942, B1-7.

Ryono, C. Robert. *Although patriotic, we were drydocked.* Los Angeles, Author, 1994.

"Terminal Island placed under Navy control; all Japanese to be moved off within 30 days." *Press-Telegram*, 13 February 1942, B1-8.

"To develop fisheries: experiments to be made by Long Beach boy." *Evening Tribune*, 27 January 1904, 1:4.

"Twenty-eight alien Japs rounded up here by FBI." *Press-Telegram*, 22 February 1942, A1-7.

"We call it Terminal Island." *Independent Press-Telegram*, 22 January 1949, Southland Magazine: 3:1.

CHAPTER 20 - Surfing
Notes:

[1] "Two lives saved by skillful use of Hawaiian surfers." *Daily Telegram*, 4 September 1911, 1:1.

[2] "Mermen without skirts barred from beach and ocean where Long Beach policemen reign." *Daily Telegram*, 25 September 1920, 9:7.

[3] "Beach guards must don skirts; scant attire condemned." *Long Beach Press*, 13 May 1921, 1:7.

Bibliography:

"Bathing suit specification duly adopted; has resulted in 30 arrests in city in past two days." *Press-Telegram*, 29 May 1932, B1-3.

Borland, "Doc". "Duke Kahanamoku shakes dust of Hawaii from his feet and makes Los Angeles his home." *Daily Telegram*, 3 September 1922, A4: 1.

"Caught in surf board: bather dragged through water by fast launch." *Daily Telegram*, 14 June 1916, 7:4.

Chilcote, Ken. "Plant run by L.B. couple scores with special suits for surf riders." *Independent Press-Telegram*, 23 Feb. 1964, R1-1.

"Haig Prieste home from three months of Hawaiian tour; has mammoth surf board given him." *Daily Telegram*, 15 August 1921, 10:3.

"Hawaiian surfriders arrive for contest." *Press-Telegram*, 22 November 1939, B1-5.

"Local boy races Hawaiian champ: Duke Kahanamoku, who visited here yesterday, appears in fast contest." *Daily Telegram*, 12 July 1913, 8:5.

"National surfboard riders seeking title." *Press-Telegram*, 16 October 1938, A7-1.

"New fad of hotel guests: wear smoked glasses because of sun." *Daily Telegram*, 6 September 1911, 4:4.

"Ordinance on bathing apparel awaiting action; another will have to do with use of surfboards." *Press-Telegram*, 28 May 1933, B1-3.

"States' celebrants take to surfboards." *Press-Telegram*, 8 August 1938, A1-4.

"Suggests use of surf boats: visitor just in from Hawaii favors new amusement for Long Beach." *Long Beach Press*, 7 April 1910, 3:3.

"Surf event is won by Hermosans: competed, won in fog." *Press-Telegram*, 4 December 1939, A7-1.

"Surf sulky on eve of board test: indications fail to offer promise of powerful breakers." *Press-Telegram*, 2 December 1939, B1-6.

"Surfboard riders must watch areas: emergency ordinance restricts use of boards to certain sections." *Press-Telegram*, 16 June 1933, B1-6.

"Surfriders watched by big crowd; award presented winning team." *Press-Telegram*, 12 December 1938, A4:3.

"Swim to island plan; local inventors of suit propose to stage race from here to Catalina Island; non-sinkable garment has ribs of air filled hose." *Long Beach Press*, 29 June 1921, 13:1.

"Swimming trunks given approval in municipal court; jury acquits two charged with wearing suits too abbreviated." *Press-Telegram*, 30 March 1932, B1:5

"Will do his stuff at Alamitos Bay: Duke Kahanamoku, water sprint champion, comes Saturday for title meet." *Long Beach Press*, 25 July 1922, C1:2.

"Woman, hurt by surfboard July 5, dies of injury: fatality first of kind ever recorded in history of beach." *Press-Telegram*, 7 July 1937, B1-5.

INDEX

Claudine Burnett is the head of the Literature and History Department of the Long Beach Public Library and a board member of the Historical Society of Long Beach. Mrs. Burnett has her B.A. in history from the University of California Irvine, an M.L.S. from the University of California Los Angeles, and an M.P.A. from California State University Long Beach. She has also been a columnist and feature writer for various journals and has written *From Barley Fields to Oil Town: A Tour of Huntington Beach 1901-1922* and *Haunted Long Beach*. She lives in Orange County California with her surfer husband and two cats..